ADVERTEASE

The Itch and the Scratch of Advertising

Mukul P Gupta

Nutshell

ADVERTEASE
The Itch and the Scratch of Advertising
By Mukul P Gupta
researchgate.net/profile/Mukul_Gupta4
linkedin.com/in/mukulpgupta
facebook.com/mukulpgupta
twitter.com/mukulpgupta

First Edition

© 2021, Mukul P Gupta

All rights reserved. This book or parts thereof may not be reproduced in any form, stored in any retrieval system, or transmitted in any form by any means—electronic, mechanical, photocopy, recording, or otherwise—without prior written permission of the author.

Limit of Liability/Disclaimer of Warranty: The author makes no representations of warranties with respect to the accuracy or completeness of the contents of this book and specifically disclaim all warranties, including without limitation warranties of fitness for a particular purpose. No warranty may be created or extended by sales or promotional materials. The advice and strategies contained herein may not be suitable for every situation. The author shall not be liable for damages arising here from. The fact that an organisation or website is referred to in this work as a citation and/or a potential source of further information does not mean that the author endorses the information the organisation or the Website may provide or recommendations it may make. Further, the reader should be aware that Internet Websites mentioned in the work might have changed or disappeared between when this work was written and when it is read.

For permission requests, write to the author at econtactmukul@gmail.com.

ISBN: 979-83-39641-55-1 (HB) ISBN: 979-85-91181-14-7 (PB)
Imprint: Independently published

NUTSHELL
Packages of intriguing and contrarian knowledge in very few words.
Other Titles in the Series:
Wisdom of Business: Simulating Business through Cases
ISBN: 979-83-39314-07-3 (HB) ISBN: 979-85-88523-74-5 (PB)

ADVERTEASE

The Itch and the Scratch of Advertising

Mukul P Gupta

Nutshell:

Packages of intriguing and contrarian knowledge in very few words.

Other Titles in the Series:

Wisdom of Business
Simulating Business through Cases
Pedagogics for Wisdom, Acumen and Literacy of Business
ISBN: 979-85-88523-74-5

*This one is for you
Papa and Mummy,
wherever you are
in the limitlessness of space and enormity of time.*

*Sunita, Varsha and Chhaya
all our dreams may come true!*

Suppose you get up early to travel to work. You are in a perfect sync with the day. You get ready, have breakfast, hop in your car, turn on the radio and start your journey. You are in a perfect flow but suddenly are stuck in a traffic jam. You spend one and a half hour stuck in a jam and finally reach your office another hour late. However, your fellow member, who wakes up late, and starts late, has still managed to reach on time just because he managed to check the traffic on the way. Bad situation right! This happens when a research is not a part of your plan and this is how advertising research becomes important for an agency to launch a campaign.

Contents

	Contents	vi
	Preface	viii
	About the author	xiv
1	**Advertising: An Inquiry into the Discipline**	1
	What is advertising!	1
	Nature of Advertising	8
	History & Development of Advertising	11
	The Purpose of Advertising	15
	Applications & Scope of Advertising	17
	Economic Issues in Advertising	21
	Social and Ethical Issues in Advertising	31
	Advertising: An Engine for Welfare	36
2	**Glitches & Hitches in Gauging Success of Advertising**	39
	Advertising Works	40
	Basic Assumptions of Professionals	44
	Excellence-Perplexity Fringe in Advertising	47
	How Advertising Works: Status of Theory	49
	Advertising Theory: Some Possibilities	69
3	**Methods of Measuring Effectiveness of Advertising**	79
	Advertising Research	81
	The Premises of Advertising Research	82
	Some Typical Advertising Effects	86
	Measuring Effectiveness of Advertising	89
	Pre-Placement Evaluation of Advertising	93
	The Media Factor	96
	Post-testing	103
	Interpretation of Research Findings	110
	Application of Effectiveness Research	111
	Improving on Effectiveness of Advertising	111

4	**A Fresh Take on Advertising Effects**	113
	Fishbein's Attitude Model	114
	An Experimental Evaluation of *Fishbein* Theory	117
	Conclusions on *Fishbein* Theory's Testing	121
	Cursors for a Different Model for Advertising Processes	125
	Communication Relevant Theories	131
	Towards a New Theory of Advertising	138
5	**Planning the Persuasive Communication**	145
	Down the Ladder of Goals, Strategies and Toolkits	145
	Publicity is not Advertising, PR is not Publicity	147
	Cheat-sheet for Marketing Communications	149
	Marketing Communications Programme	151
	Segmentation and Positioning	152
	Positioning Strategy	154
	Setting Objectives for Advertising	154
	Brand Personality	157
	Benefits Based Attitudes	158
	Developing a Communication Brief	160
	Advertising Appropriations and Budgets	161
6	**Creating and Delivering Advertisements**	165
	Creative Strategy Elements	166
	Brand Communications	174
	Media Strategy	180
	Media Classes	184
	Media Planning	197
	Direct Response Communications – Database Marketing	205
	Sales Promotions	208
	Consumer Promotions	209
	Trade Promotions	210
	Public Relations	210
	Retail Advertising	212
	B2B Advertising	213
	Non-profit or Social Marketing	213
	References	215

Preface

Not having a well-developed body of advertising theory, both theoreticians and practitioners of advertising, make assumptions about the chain of events that take place between advertisement exposures and resulting audience behaviour.

The advertising practitioner, in the creation of advertisements, moves through a reasonably determined and common series of professional steps. Inherent in these professional steps is the belief that if they are followed, the resulting advertisements will be effective in increasing the probability that those people, who are exposed to them, will behave or think as the advertiser wishes them to do.

The basic question here could be stated as -- "How Advertising Works?" The answer to this question has eluded academics, psychologists, marketing or advertising practitioners and even the sociologists or anthropologists for long. It appears possible to divide the main current, theoretical formulations of the advertising process into four; Pressure-Response Theories; Active-Learning Theories; Low-Involvement Theories; and Dissonance-Reduction Theories

All the four streams of thought in advertising suggest that there is no consensus about how consumers interact with advertising and how these specific interactions lead to particular results in the market place. Most theorists are trying to believe that there are only three elements in the process, that is, learning sequence, attitude change and behaviour change and any attempt to explain the process of advertising effects has only to establish the right sequence of these three elements is only unfortunate.

Advertising needs to be viewed as a marketing tool that performs a necessary balancing function by synchronizing the process of mass consumption. We are now a knowledge economy with productive operations of mass processes. On a macro basis, advertising reduces the time between production and consumption by joining the technology of communications with the technology of manufacture.

In all the frameworks, advertising is viewed as having a cause-effect relationship. This is inadequate as discrepancies are bound to exist between what the advertiser presents in an ad. (Copy, visual, messages or execution) and the information and meaning audience derive out of it. This can be attributed to the complexity of the needs, emotions, values and a host of other such elements of the audience.

Let us, for a while, ignore the questions like - how advertising

- affects the macro-economy
- shapes society, its values, beliefs or aspirations
- Works as a means of mass communication for wider purposes like social goals, charity, good-cause or idea-propagation.

Such questions are better left to the economists, sociologists and anthropologists to advise us upon.

Instead, let us treat advertising as a promotional tool strategically employed by marketing organisations towards attainment of their marketing and business goals. Let us limit our interest in answering this question as to - How Advertising works such that

- it could be used as a marketing tool by a business firm;
- it helps in achieving of marketing objectives of the firm;

- its usage over time could give sustained competitive advantage to the firm, and
- it interacts with other elements of marketing-mix towards attainment of common goals.

The managerial approach that is being taken up here is that effectiveness is a function of how the process is conceptualised. Advertising effects are being taken as a binding glue or a system of information that causes the congruence in the three distinct images in the mind of the customer, viz., the customer's self image; the brand's image and the product's source image. Since advertising, like marketing, is meant for the mutual benefits of buyers and sellers, efforts would be necessary to upgrade, modify in quality and quantity, and design advertising in a way that it becomes more and correlatively informative and binding.

The success of this approach could lead to gains in the following areas:

- Increase in gains per rupee spent on advertising.
- Decrease in rupees spent per unit of item sold or consumed.
- Decrease in time and effort spent by a consumer in seeking information for pre-purchase evaluation.
- Better estimation of likely effects of any advertisement or a campaign.
- Understanding the phenomenon and process of mass communication so far as it applies to marketing
- Building a theory of advertising.
- Reduction in time lag between technology, mass production and consumption.
- Elimination or reduction in waste in production and consumption.

This approach is derived from the marketing framework that suggests that there are some potential customers who have needs and they have the willingness and ability to pay for the satisfaction of those needs. Business enterprises see an opportunity in such potential customers. They offer products to these customers. Considering the mutual perceptions of the gains made through the transaction, the business-customer interaction is sustained, grows or fades away.

Advertising is used as a tool by the enterprise in this interaction -

- to inform customer that a product exists for his needs.
- to persuade customer that he could look forward to satisfaction of his needs through the offering
- to stimulate customer to buy and consume the offering
- to make customer realise the gains accruing to him out of this interaction
- to motivate customer to sustain these interactions.

Nevertheless, the enterprise uses some other tools simultaneously for these interactions. It uses product design, features, attributes, packaging, branding, pricing, channels of distribution, personal selling, etc. for this very purpose.

Therefore, what does advertising do really and how it accomplishes it? Is advertising complementary to all such efforts or it supplements them? Since the unit of interaction between the enterprise and the customer is an exchange of product for a price, what is the framework for exchange? This is to say-

- What are the conditions necessary for an exchange to take place?
- What are the conditions sufficient for the exchange to take place?

- What are the conditions under which the exchange would be repeated?
- When would the exchange not be repeated?
- Can a sustained exchange be disrupted? If yes, under what conditions?
- How can another exchange take place when the outcome of earlier exchange ruled out a repeat exchange?
- What is the role of advertising in exchange process?
- How does this role change in the various exchange situations listed above?

A completely new way of looking at advertising is presented here. This new look approach makes use of the idea of images in the minds of people, images which are richer than a photo-picture in terms of its dimensions and dynamism.

The first image is SELF IMAGE, an image that one has about oneself. An image that one carries of a brand is called as BRAND IMAGE. Again, the person uses ones experience, knowledge, learning, surroundings, location, stocking patterns etc. to form images about the source of supply for the product. This image is called the SOURCE IMAGE. The three images are independent of each other.

The entire gambit of customers' response to marketing programmes of an organisation has to relate to these three images, viz., Brand Image, Self-Image and Source Image. When the customer finds some kind of a harmony or congruence between the three images, sales happen.

Advertising shapes the three images. Advertising works through image congruence. Extent of congruence results in varying advertising effects.

This approach may not be revolutionary, yet it helps in changing some of the problems that prevent our understanding of the advertising phenomenon properly. The elimination altogether of these problems may still be very far away.

This is the second in the "**Nutshell**" series of books, which are packages of intriguing and contrarian knowledge in very few words. I hope the reader would acquire wisdom by reading them, reflecting upon them and putting them to test.

With this hope, that the readers would like to crack open more "*Nutshells*" in their pursuit for worldly wisdom, I present to them this second "**Nutshell**" as I promise to keep bringing them more.

गुरुग्राम Gurugram
मकर संक्रांति, पौष, शुक्ल पक्ष प्रतिपदा
Makar Sankranti, Pausa, Shukla Paksha Pratipada
जनवरी 14, 2021, गुरुवार, विक्रम संवत 2077
January 14, 2021, Thursday, Vikram Samvat 2077

मुकुल प्र गुप्ता
Mukul P Gupta

About the author

Mukul P Gupta is a Professor of Marketing & Management. He took his basic degree in physical sciences in 1979. He is a Gold Medallist in the MBA programme of 1981 from the University of Rajasthan, Jaipur. His doctoral work has been in the area of advertising effectiveness.

In a career, that spans 40 years, he spent over 10-years in industry, marketing and Advertising, and the rest in academics. He has been to 30 countries spread over five continents for professional engagements. He has served as head of a premier business school in South Africa and another leading business school in India.

His current academic interests are in the areas of Strategy, Communications, and Consumer Reactions. He engages with international organisations and Indian enterprises assisting them in making wiser decisions.

He serves on various committees and leadership teams of academic institutions and accreditation bodies spread across the world.

Mukul lives in Gurgaon, which now has a new name, Gurugram, the largest city in Haryana, since the turn of the millennium, 2 decades back.

1

Advertising: An Inquiry into the Discipline

If all the emotion advertising has stirred, all the actions it has provoked, all the hypnotism it has exerted and all the gullibility it has evoked could be added up, the sum would approximate the dimensions of total human nature.

> *"There are a lot of great technicians in advertising. And unfortunately, they talk the best game. They know all the rules ... but there's one little rub. They forget that advertising is persuasion, and persuasion is not a science, but an art. Advertising is the art of persuasion."* – **William Bernbach**

What is advertising!

That advertising exists in obvious to all who can see or hear. That advertising does things in apparent on the balance sheets of companies, in the lovely solvency of advertising agencies, in the food people eat, the clothes they wear, the kind of houses they live in, the cars or motor bikes they ride and in many of their most firmly embedded and other baseless assumptions. Advertising refuses to be made into a science and has never purely been an art. What then is advertising? People have come up with various ideas and explanations to the concept of advertising.

Salesmanship in Print

From the beginning of his spectacular career in advertising, something in the nature of the redoubtable Albert Davis Lasker (1953) made it necessary for him to know what the force he successfully applied actually was. He decided and formulated a working definition; *"Advertising is news"*. That understanding worked well enough for Lasker in the 1890's.

Then he seized on another that changed his whole concept of what he was doing and changed fundamentally much of the advertising of the next 20 years. In a Chicago saloon in 1899, John E Kennedy (1905) told Lasker *"Advertising is salesmanship in Print."* It was a revelation.

Supreme Flowering of a Sophisticated Civilisation

In 1905, another advertising man, Earnest Elmo Calkins (1924) who was to become a famous copy writer, tried to put down all the things that he thought advertising was:

> *"Advertising is a great, though almost unknown force made up of a hundred different elements, each one too intangible to be defined. It is something which properly directed, becomes a powerful agency in influencing human customs and manners. All the great forces that have moved the race, the eloquence of the orator, the fervour of the religious enthusiast, superstition, panic, terror, hypnotism, all these are used in advertising. All the emotions of the race are played upon, appealed to, coaxed, cultivated and utilised. The man who can tell most nearly what one thousand people*

will think upon a given topic will come nearest to producing successful advertising, but no human being can foretell the actual results of any advertising that ever was planned."

Nineteen years later, he could be briefer. In 1924 he concluded, "Advertising is the supreme flowering of a sophisticated civilisation."

The Five Essentials

"Salesmanship in print" was soon under attack as a satisfactory definition of advertising. Arthur Brisbane said that advertising was not selling at all; it was merely *"telling"*. *"A good advertisement must do five things and do them all. If it fails in one, it fails in all. It must make people see it, read it, understand it, believe it, want it."*

"Advertising is making people think as you desire. It means introducing all those forces, which produce impressions and crystallise opinion... The great power of advertisements is in getting into people's minds the ideas that they carry in such a way that people think they always had them."

Greer concludes that *"anything is advertisement whether communicated by printing or otherwise to absent persons which conveys to them knowledge where a product may be obtained and conveys it in such a way as to cause them to desire it."*

In the Eyes of the Psychologist

In October 1895, Printers' Ink had stated editorially that eventually the advertising writer, like the teacher, would have to study psychology, for "The advertising writer and the teacher have one great object in common to influence the human mind." Printer's Ink had urged again in March 1901 that the advertising writer should have a working knowledge of psychology. Scott noted both these comments in the introduction to a small book, "**The Psychology of Advertising**", which, privately printed, appeared first in 1902 as "**The Theory and Practice of Advertising**", but carried the better-known and more accurate title in later editions.

Scott (1908) applied pre-Freudian psychology to advertising in chapters on memory suggestion, human instincts, habit, the feelings and emotions, the will and what he called as the "laws of progressive thinking". He said at one point, "An advertisement has not accomplished its mission till it has instructed the possible customer concerning the goods and then has caused him to forget where have received his instruction."

In 1909, George French strained to pin down the actuality of advertising in a book, which referred to pragmatism, the conscious and the unconscious mind. French came bravely to the not very illuminating conclusion that advertising was, "personality with knowledge working upon personality with needs."

In 1923, George French tried once more to capture the essential meaning of advertising:

> "The peculiar appeal that is made to people to buy something or to do something, which is called advertising, is a functioning of salesmanship and propaganda not discovered in any other use of persuasive power and language. It is something apart, which cannot be defined by reference or analogy. It is in the nature of a connecting link between the spoken language and the written argument, taking on the persuasive power of the

former and adding to it the descriptive qualities of the later... It is a personal appeal through impersonal mediums... It is a hybrid in the field of expression, desired to effect results impossible by other methods... It is a great power for good, which is often employed in attempting evil."

Academia's Forays into Theorising

Academia had noted the phenomena, which for centuries had been the possession and accomplishment of the vulgar. Solemn consideration of advertising seems to have crept into academic thought through a new subject, which, in most conservative intellectual circles of the time, was not seen to be too reputable. As the serious study of advertising developed, more and more attempts were made to embalm the quickness and form-less extravagance of advertising in the formal language of chill abstraction.

New York University established its Advertising Division in 1913. Two years later, four faculty members who had helped found and develop the division wrote a book, which, they made very clear in their preface, would embody their two years' experience and once for all, put everything that was known about the principles, psychology and application of advertising into its proper place. *"Advertising"*, the four decided, *"is the application of the force of publicity to the sale of commodities or services by increasing the public knowledge and desire for the items specified therein."* *"It was"*, they added, *"in reality the machine or bulk method of selling."*

Walter Dill Scott, an associate professor in psychology, became the president of North Western University in 1920 and paid attention to advertising. Largely though this circumstance, advertising became a subject of interest to the psychologist before it became, as it did later, a major concern of the economist.

Politicians' Views on Advertising

Politicians, especially when they are seeking favour through advertising, can also be eloquent about advertising and its virtues. Franklin D. Roosevelt, in a letter of June 15, 1933 to the Advertising Federation of America described advertising as *"an economic and social force of vital importance."* On other occasion he declared, "If I were starting my life over again, I am inclined to think, I would go into the advertising business in preference to almost any other."

In sonorous rhetoric, England's most colourful modern prime minister, Sir Winston Churchill declaimed, *"Advertising nourishes the consuming power of men. It creates wants for a better standard of living. It sets up before a man the goal of better home, better clothing, better food for himself and his family. It spurs individual exertion and greater production. It brings together in fertile union, those things which otherwise would never have met."*

Sir Thomas Lipton (1931), artful and indefatigable practitioner of advertising in a thousand forms, tells of a famous Victorian prime minister, William Enart Gladstone's uttering in a speech in Edinburgh:
> *"Advertising is to business what steam is to industry, the sole propelling power. Nothing except the mint can make money without advertising."*

Though he did not credit his source, Gladstone was quoting an earlier advertising authority, Thomas Babington Macaulay. Gladstone read American magazines not for editorial content, but for their advertising. It was in American magazine advertising, he said, that he saw reflected the growth of the United States.

Touch-me-not Attitude of Advertising Professionals

Advertising man are a little shocked at ruthless dispatches from businesspersons just as they are somewhat chilled by the cold conclusions of the academics. They prefer longer and more eloquent descriptions of their dedicated endeavours. Advertising to them is not just news, salesmanship in print, telling, notification, indirect selling, publicity, suggestion, "Systematic Instruction", appeal, contact, multiple communication, a "force" or a "something". It is a religious conviction, a "way of life", a drive, a fascination and a mystery.

There is another reason advertising men quail at the limit of unfriendly criticism. Standard decorum frowns on a man boasting loudly of his powers and possessions. Advertising men are professional boasters of 'the virtues of others and what they have to sell.' The principal can live at peace with his modesty, looking slightly askance at the braggart antics of his feelings. It is even a little worse than that. Advertising is a mercenary. Its services are always for hire. It has no sustained loyalties. It cannot afford them. Any good advertising agency can turn expertly from praise of one incomparable shampoo or matchless automobile to the equally deft and sincere praise of its chief competitor, which then becomes truly incomparable or matchless. Skilled advertising can un-convert, then reconvert, those, it has just converted carefully and completely.

Awareness of the parasitic nature of their trade together with conviction of its importance and knowledge of its tremendous power may be part of the reason for the hypersensitiveness of many advertising men to even the mildest of criticisms. Often they try to forestall the criticism by loud justification before the attack is launched. There are of course, other reasons for their defensiveness.

Nature of Advertising

In assaying any or all definitions and attempts at definitions, the rather baffled attempts to describe and explain, it is only fair to recognise the basic difficulty faced by anyone who tries to capture and bind advertising in logical terms. Advertising has no independent existence of its own. Advertising is nothing of itself, and it produces nothing, not even the smoke from one ballyhooed cigarette or the bubbles from one cake of rhapsodically described soap.

The Catalytic Nature

Advertising must be given an external creation, a product, service, or idea originating with some other agency, in order to exist and function. It is never an independent entity, only a concomitant noise. Even where it is most successful, in transfer of a horse, a washing machine, a world cruise, a social creed, or a political prejudice is triumphantly effected, advertising achieves no actuality of its own. At its worst, advertising is an excrescence. At its best, it is a catalyst.

Poetry like Nature

Like poetry, and there are many ways in which advertising can be looked upon as part of the poetry of human life in the twentieth century, advertising is persuasion largely through words in printed symbols of sound, sounds that when read or spoken are symbols of meaning or, more often, of fantasy. Like poetry, the appeal of most advertising is emotional.

It cannot be defended or explained by arithmetic. Unlike poetry, advertising is not disinterested art. It is sharply interested artisanship. Its purpose, as some of those whose advertising sentiments have been reviewed flatly stated, is profit, profit of some kind; and the world while furiously engaged in the activity, and charmingly persists in disdaining the pursuit.

Response Evoking Nature

No understanding of what advertising is or does can be complete that does not take into consideration people and their response to advertising. The response may sometimes be of boredom but then theirs is still a response.

There sometimes seems a convention in the conduct of advertising almost as set as the movement in a formal dance. The advertisement announces itself as an advertisement. Implicit in its existence is the declaration that it intends to defraud. There is an understood pretension. The advertisement pretends to offer more than it asks, while both parties know that the greater benefits are meant to accrue to the advertiser. Advertising in its approach must hide its confidence that it always (well, usually) wins.

Etiquette prescribes an attitude on the part of the consumer too. He must retreat as the advertisement approaches. He must not admit to instant interest, he must show indifference, a suspicion, sometimes a defiance, hide his willingness to succumb. The advertisement pretends and appeals to his reason; appeal is undisguisedly to his desires or his dreams.

The advertising approach may be warm and impetuous, diffident or as subtle as a ten penny nail though the skull. It can scream, "*Look at me"*. It can assume instead a sensitive shyness *"I hope you won't notice me or will forgive me if you do."* This too is understood. An advertisement may glow with arch innocence, shrink with modesty, or boastfully parade its muscles. It may provoke a cry of rage or pain, a movement of avoidance, a whimper of delight. It does not much matter. The challenge has been accepted. The consumer knows that he flirts with danger but he has taken the dare. Surrender is inevitable. At first, it may be only the surrender of a little attention, a shade of disbelief. Eventually, complete capitulation will come. Under stress, man or woman may forget his own name. He will not forget the name of the car, the soap, the cigarette, the dogma, the impressions somehow received.

"Every time a message seems to grab us, and we think, 'I just might try it,' we are at the nexus of choice and persuasion that is advertising." – Andrew Hacker (2010).

Irrational Nature

Often the genesis of advertising is as irrational as the appeals it employs. Advertising does not always start with deliberate cupidity, market surveys; statistically forecast sales potentials, and all the other impedimenta of the modern advertising agency approach. Many times someone is fierily convinced that he has produced something that is living and beautiful. Everyone should know of it; everyone should have it. One may not be able to distinguish it from a thousand comparable objects more prosaically hatched, but he can, and he burns to educate the ignorant to appreciation.

Advertising has one constant upon which advertiser, medium and agency can always depend. That constant is the enduring and endearing susceptibility of people.

The Enigmatic Nature

Advertising is a tale, a folk tale as well as a venture in commerce. Many people, through the centuries, best know it from wide experience of it. Inability to isolate logically the essence of advertising detracts not one whit from its vigour, not a decibel from its fury or a fraction from its force.

Perhaps advertising is not and has never been the stuff for limiting in too tight a frame. Nothing comes from nothing. You must continuously feed the inner beast that sparks and inspires. We need to stop interrupting what people are interested in and be what people are interested in. A. D. Lasker had no definition in the end. He had lived advertising furiously and well and for a long time. It was part of him and he was part of it. "Advertising", he breathed, "is a talent. It is born in you like singing or it is not. You have it or you haven't. It is conceived in the mother's womb...."

History & Development of Advertising

Perhaps, marking of products with signatures, impressions or imprints of the artists and craftsmen, who made them, is the oldest form of advertising.

The following discussion draws on Evans, 1974; Foster, 1967 and Wright et. al., 1977 -

The very beginnings of the recorded history from the early Mediterranean civilisations (nations of Sumer or Sumeria on the alluvial planes of rives Tigris and Euphrates later called Babylon, now Iraq) confirm that on the unearthed shards, bricks and tiles are the signatures and imprints of the artisans who made them.

This thus, was the mode of permanently identifying the origin of such products, and telling those who saw them, where to come back for more.

The distinction between an art and a craft was not then a very clear one, nor did it become any clearer for a very long time. This tradition of signing the finished product has continued down the centuries from pre classical times, through the great sculptures of fifth and fourth century utensils and chinaware. All these things proclaim the identity of their maker, some in pride and some for profit, but they all *"Advertise"* in the modern sense of the term (first employed by Shakespeare meaning, *"to bring to the notice"*).

In Ancient Rome

It is in classical times that are to be found the first instances of poster advertising consisting sometimes of commercial publicity for household services but mostly of political propaganda and personal insults. Visitors to Pompeii can see, as clean and as legible as on the day it was written 1900 years ago, an exhortation daubed on a wall in bold red letters to vote for Furius, who was standing for political office and who, as is said was a 'good man'.

In the internecine squabbles which punctuated the last years of the Roman Republic, the warring factions (such as the followers of Clodius and Milo, immortalised by Cicero) would conduct their battles not only with the sword but also the pen (or rather the paint brush) plastering the city buildings with their choicest insults.

Roman trade announcements give a very clear idea of the types of commerce conducted at the time, but perhaps the most famous of all are the notices advertising forthcoming public entertainments, in particular the gladiatorial combats so dear to the Roman heart and pre-empting by centuries the gay and dramatic bill posting of modern Spanish Corridas.

Ancient Rome supplies the first `Commercial break'. M. Porcius Cato, elected censor in 184 BC conducted in the senate his own personal publicity programme for the destruction of Carthage, which, in his opinion, represented a constant threat to the safety of Rome. Whatever the subject under debate, Cato ended every speech he made with the words "Delenda est carthago" (Carthage must be destroyed) before resuming his seat. His campaign was effective: the Romans eventually razed the city to the ground.

The First Printing Process

The practice and purpose of advertising changed very little in the first 1500 years AD. The reason is not hard to find. No advances were made in the two prime areas, which constitutes both the possibility, and necessity of advertising practices on the one hand, means of mass communication, on the other, the need to employ it.

The possibility was provided by the invention of printing, which represented the major extension of the opportunity to advertise communications could at last be conducted on the grand scale, the same message could be reproduced hundreds, thousands of times and its audience could be broadened immeasurably. The new printing process gave rise to the newspaper, first on a local and limited, and then on a national and unlimited scale. As well as newspapers came pamphlets, circular and posters, leaflets, broadsheets and tracts. The communications industry had been born.

Extension of Horizons

Advertising, then at last had extended its horizons further than the eye could see. The possibilities had been created, but it was not until the great upheaval in industry at the end of the eighteenth and the beginning of the nineteenth century that the necessity to advertise arose on a scale never previously envisaged.

The industrial revolution produced the real ingredients of the modern sales and marketing operation; first, the production of goods in mass quantity; secondly, the need for mass distribution to enable these goods to be sold; and thirdly, the need for mass communication to promote their qualities and thus facilitate the selling process.

It is really from this time that one could begin to measure the growth of the bread and butter of advertising packaged goods and the emergence of the system selling process.

The First Agency

It is a curious fact and perhaps unique to advertising, that the way in which the modern advertising agency operates is in essence identical to that which was put into practice in the first agency to be created.

It is to an American, Volney Palmer in 1841, that the credit for founding the first agency must go. He was a dealer in real estate, wood, coal and other commodities in Philadelphia and at the same time he solicited advertising revenue for a number of local newspapers in New Jersey and Pennsylvania. This side of his business developed rapidly; he made it quite clear to his `clients' that the newspapers were his `principals' and that he was their `agent.

His clients were charged no more for their advertising space than if they had bought it direct from the newspaper, and Palmer was paid an agreed commission by the newspaper. He was very successful and soon had branches in other cities including New York, Boston and Baltimore, but it is doubtful whether, successful as he was, he ever realised that he had founded a totally new industry.

The Golden Age - Growth of the Agency

The early ad. Agencies, almost in spite of themselves, were forced into the situation of having to provide their clients with a *Complete* service, consisting of both creative material and media buying even through no payment for creative services was made. The preparation of advertisement content was from the beginning, part of the service, paid for (oddly enough) not by the client but by the publication. In the years to come, agencies were to rue the day that such terms of business had ever been permitted.

A new trend has emerged where limited service advertising agencies like those specialising in only media buying, or advertising writing or advertising production have emerged and threatened the full service advertising agencies in terms of cost efficiency and expertise. Some advertisers have also begun to form their own in house agencies and the seeds for in-house agencies and boutique agencies were sown.

The Purpose of Advertising

Advertising has both forward and backward linkages in the process of satisfaction across the entire spectrum of human needs.

The explicit function of advertising is to make people aware of the existence of the product, service or idea, which would help them, fulfil their felt need and spell out the differential benefits in a competitive situation.

On advertising also lies the onus, at least marginally, of motivating the prospects to strive for creation of resources for fulfilling the new needs, or in the alternative to serve as an aid for reallocation of available resources.

Therefore, advertising is not merely directed at selling, or achieving the objective of gaining acceptance for a worthwhile idea or programme, it may also be an instrument of developing the basic motivation for creating resources for buying goods and services or generating favourable conditions for the acceptance of an idea.

From Fig Leaf to Furs

Dwelling for a while on the motivational construct, which after all is the foundation of human progress, the advertiser and the support system namely advertising agency and media have only a very limited role. Social scientists gave advertising a form and focus, using the basis of psychology against the background of socio economic norms. Marketing men, being quick at the uptake, assimilated the advertising concept swiftly and adopted it as a part of marketing mix.

Perhaps, advertising came first and marketing followed. Surely, there can be no marketing transaction without meaningful communication and that is what marketing is all about, from the fig leaf to furs and well beyond. Needs escalate, consumer perceptions of products and services change and norms of presentation are modified and adapted accordingly. Buyers' attitudes towards products would be determined not merely by products as manufactured in factories, but also by what is added in the form of packaging, services, advertising, customer advice, financing, delivery arrangements, warehousing and other things that people value.

Applications & Scope of Advertising

It is useful to realise that the functions of advertising have a specific role to play as a marketing input. This role is obviously relevant in the context of marketing of all types of goods and services and concern manufacturers and marketers. Selling of space and time by media also requires advertising support and one can see evidence of such advertising in countries like India, where the media field has become competitive.

Advertising is an all pervasive fact of most growing communities. It has important consequences for the advertisers who use it individuals who are exposed to it. However, its economic and social impact is a subject of continuous controversy.

The following aspects illustrate the basic modes of applications of advertising:

Communication with Consumers

There is an increasing need for information concerning a variety of products as an economy expands and grows more complex. Advertising is the major way of establishing communication between manufactures and other organisations providing services or trying to put across ideas and concepts on the one hand, and customers and buyers and potential acceptors on the other. Advertising is a reminder to the existing consumers and it aims at cultivating new prospects as well. Advertising, therefore, has been described as `Effective Communication' with the target audience.

Consumers need information about various goods and services. Due to ignorance, a consumer may purchase an inferior product, pay higher prices or not even know that the product exists.

Persuasion

Advertising attempts to persuade prospective buyers into buying a product/service. All success in business and industry and similar activities depends upon the process of planned persuasion. In modern markets, the producer who is content with advertising that merely identifies or informs may soon find himself in a vulnerable position. The consumer should be aware of the advertiser's persuasive interest, no matter how restrained and informative the message may be.

Brand Image Building

Very often, advertising is used to build brand image. Images are metal pictures of brands that may appeal to different segments of audience in varying degree. These may be based on real or assumed features. The images projected are often geared to match the needs and the expectations of the target audiences. Favourable images will help in generating brand loyalty and a disposition to buy that brand in preference to another brand of the product required.

Innovation

Advertising is seen to perform this task most effectively for new products. In a way, it reduces the risk of innovation. The cost of innovation can be more than recouped because of the sales that advertising the innovation could generate and this encourages manufacturers to undertake research and development.

The brand launches seem to abound in the toiletry, the cosmetic, the pharmaceutical, the confectionery and the tobacco market, which are usually characterised by heavy advertising. Nevertheless, at the same time, it should be pointed out that advertising does not guarantee success to all new products.

New Product Launch

Producers often attempt to modify their products to fit the special needs, which they have perceived amongst a group of potential buyers. Various strategies including advertising are then employed to make such buyers aware of the products and convince them of their suitability.

The term 'new product' may include modifications of existing products, limitations of competitive products and product line acquisitions. The firm may follow whatever policy; advertising usually bears a large proportion of the responsibility for informing the public about the attributes of the new products. Thus, advertising can help introduce new products, call attention to changes in old products and weld together a family of products made by the same manufacturer. Advertising causes people to want things that are available to them. It helps people to overcome old habits by successfully introducing to them the new products available.

Non Business Advertising

Advertising is concerned with much more than the promotion of tangible goods. Although the primary use of advertising has been to help sell goods and commercial services, it is now also being used increasingly to further public interest, and goods and services with limited or little profit motive. The Indian Cancer Society ran an advertising campaign in 1979-80. The theme centred around a positive approach to an otherwise fearful disease and gave valuable information on facilities for regular check-ups.

This campaign was highly successful and was applauded as a professional masterpiece. It became a subject for a case at the Indian Institute of Management, Ahmedabad, which this author was fortunate to write along with late Prof. Manendra Mohan in 1982.

Advertising has been widely used in non-commercial ventures also. For example, in political campaigns, candidates use banners, outdoor signs and newspaper advertising. In several countries, where there is commercial television, the candidates can buy time for electioneering. In India, Advertising has been widely used to spread literacy, to campaign against atrocities on *Harijans*, to secure financial support for charitable causes, to generate public conviction for national integration and communal harmony, and to achieve many other non-commercial objectives.

The word 'idea', very often, can be substituted for the word `product'. Advertising strategy for selling ideas such as conservation of energy and similar socially desirable aims can be evolved using the same basic principles as those used for tangible products. As for example, of late, the Petroleum Conservation Research Association has been advertising continuously for saving fuel by giving various suggestions for using less fuel in cooking. Similarly, anti-vehicular pollution campaigns, safe driving practices campaign, donation for the relief campaigns, are all examples of this kind. Latest campaign on safety measures from corona pandemic joins the polio vaccination and aids-awareness campaigns in areas of public health.

Economic Issues in Advertising

Questions have often been raised about the effects of advertising on consumer welfare and the functioning of the economic system. Of late, this subject has assumed great importance due to a growing consumer movement. A lobby of public opinion considers expenditure on advertising wasteful and an increase in advertising expenditure undesirable. To some of them, advertising is the cheapest way of selling goods, particularly if the goods are worthless.

Advertising supports the core principles that shaped our nation: free speech, competition, and democracy. Since colonial times, advertising has provided a source of vital information about our open, market-based economy. Two Nobel Laureates in economics, Dr. Kenneth Arrow and the late Dr. George Stigler (1994), praise the value of advertising: *"Advertising is a powerful tool of competition. It provides valuable information about products and services in an efficient and cost-effective manner. In this way, advertising helps the economy to function smoothly—it keeps prices low and facilitates the entry of new products and new firms into the market."*

A 1999 study by one of the country's premier econometric modelling firms, the WEFA Group, and Nobel Laureate in economics Dr. Lawrence R. Klein further underscored this economic impact. The study found that advertising played a key role in generating 18.2 million of the 126.7 million jobs in the United States in that year. The report further concluded that advertising expenditures contributed between 12 and 16 percent of private sector revenues throughout the country, in rural as well as urban areas.

A later study, conducted in 2005 by the financial analysis firm Global Insight, demonstrated that advertising helps to generate more than

$5.2 trillion in sales and economic activity throughout the U.S. economy annually. That represents 20 percent of the nation's $25.5 trillion in total economic activity. This economic stimulus provided support throughout the economy for more than twenty-one million jobs, or 15.2 percent of the U.S. workforce.

The purpose of the study was to quantify the economic and employment impacts of advertising. The study removed intervening effects (like consumers simply buying a product to replace an old one or a depleted one) to measure the role of advertising itself.

Business Environment and Advertising

A study conducted by the Strategic Planning Institute (SPI) indicates the utility of advertising in periods of economic recession.

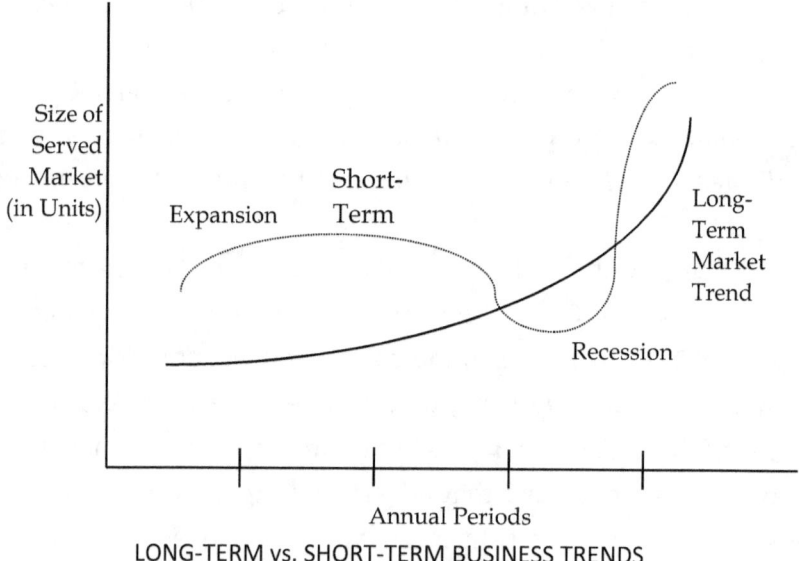

LONG-TERM vs. SHORT-TERM BUSINESS TRENDS

Recession according to this study refers to periods of sluggish economic and industrial activity when the rate of growth of the market served is substantially lower than the long-term trend. Deviations of short-term trends from the long market trend indicate periods of expansion and recession.

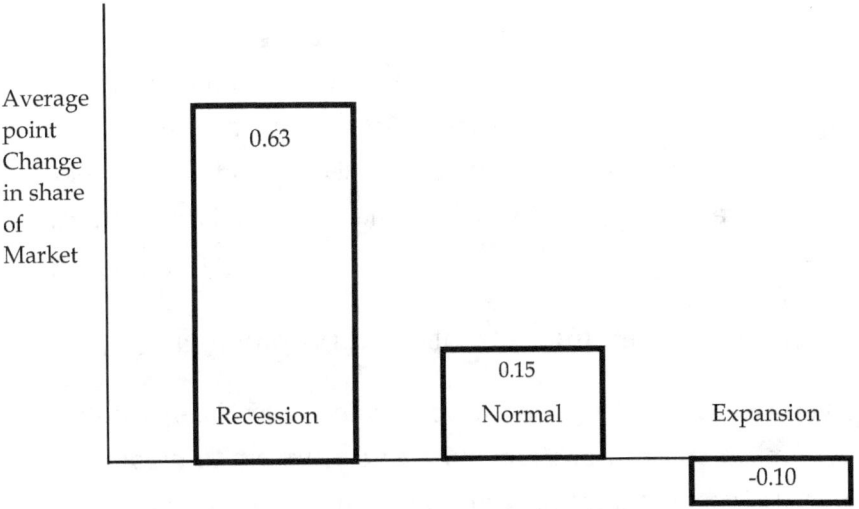

AVERAGE INDUSTRIAL BUSINESS MARKET SHARE
AFFECTED BY MARKET CONDITIONS

The analysis of the PIMS data showed that during recessionary periods, average business recorded gains in their market share apparently at the expense of smaller competitors and those who were less willing to defend themselves. During expansion periods, however, some businesses have difficulty in meeting the growing demand allowing competitors an easier entry into the market.

Another study by the Laboratory of Advertising Performance indicated that companies, which maintained or increased their advertising expenditures during the global recession period of 1974-75, had greater sales growth than those companies, which reduced such expenditures. There is a famous quote from two marketing Gurus, Britt & Boyd (1978) *"Doing business without advertising is like winking at a girl in the dark. You know what you are doing, but nobody else does."*

Effect on Business Cycles

Advertising could be a tool for alleviating the extremes of business cycles. When an economy is in a relatively recessionary phase, some firms increase their advertising. This may have the effect of expediting purchase decisions, especially for industrial products, machinery and plant, and thus diminishing the amplitude of business cycles.

Increases in Economic Activity and Employment

Advertising and selling may have played a part in expanding the economic system through stimulating consumers to greater effort. Advertising and aggressive selling have led people to want things and to get the desired products.

They have been induced to work harder than they would otherwise. This has had the effect of raising the level of production of goods and services in the economy.

From a long range point of view, aggressive selling and advertising have probably played a considerable part in making people favourably disposed towards high levels of consumption and an acceptance of new products and new ideas.

Increases in Standards of Living

Advertising contributes to economic growth by helping to expand markets, particularly for new products and by helping to develop new market segments.

Advertising also helps in lowering prices by reducing per unit costs of production and distribution.

Advertising encourages mass consumption and consequently it may lead to substantial increase in production. This enables manufacturers to reap the benefits of the economies of scale. Since the cost of production per unit is brought down, it lowers the prices and consumers are benefited. This has been the long-term experience of a number of industrial nations.

An obvious objective of advertising is to influence prospects favourably towards the products and services advertised. This is commonly termed as the `pull' effect, which can thus help in reducing the cost of distribution.

A study by Steiner (1973) indicated that there was a substantial decline in the retailer's margin as well as consumer prices of toys between 1955 and 1970 in the USA. Advertising can be a motivating factor for the less privileged, who may be induced to some extent by advertising to make additional efforts and seek opportunities for increasing their purchasing power.

With increasing motivation for acquisition of products coupled with becoming available within the reach of poor due to lowering of prices, standards of living begin to rise.

Guide to Prospective Buyers

Advertising is an instrument of persuasion and information. The informative Role of advertisements consists in provision of information about products, their specification, features and functions and prices to prospective buyers.

"Conventional demand theory endows the consumer with a vast amount of information. The consumer is held knowledgeable of the configuration of attributes that comprise a product or a service. Further, he is assumed to be aware of the product price alternatives available to him and has well defined taste and preferences and can determine his marginal rate of substitution for each product for the other possible alternative products involved in a particular purchases decision." - Tull, Boring and Gonsior (1964)

In life, however, consumers would not be as well informed. Kaldor (1950) observes that if advertisements were not provided free, consumers would be quite willing to pay for the supply of information.

Primary and Selective Demand

Stopping advertising to save money is like stopping your watch to save time. The demand for a class of product as a whole may be termed primary demand and the demand of individual companies; selective demand.

Borden points out that advertising may shift the demand for a class of product when the demand for that product is expandable i.e. subject to increase through appeals to consumers' buying motives.

In influencing the shape of the demand curve for any type or class of products, advertising may make the demand either more elastic or less elastic.

If a company is able to shift its demand curve with the help of advertising, it will attain a larger share of the industry's total sales unless primary demand expands in equal ratio.

Propensity to Consume

There can be two hypotheses according to Simon about the effect of advertising on the propensity to consume-

a) advertising does effect aggregate spending;

b) advertising does no more than affect how people allocate the budgeted amount.

The considerable stability in the average propensity to consume over many decades is consistent with an allocation hypothesis. Advertising affects the long run propensity to consume by affecting tastes though it is doubtful that the impact could occur rapidly as to affect spending over a business cycle. On the other hand, advertising might affect the short run propensity to consume by informing consumers of bargains.

Higher propensity to consume may be formed on the following grounds:

a) Consumption stimulates productivity because people feel motivated to work harder and earn more in order to satisfy their needs. This extra effort on their part also increases productivity and helps develop economy.

b) Secondly, advertising for mass consumption goods can help in gradually reducing disparities and breaking barriers as those between the urban elite and others by making more products available in rural areas.

Raising the propensity to consume can be undesirable as it can lead to conspicuous consumption. Thus, money can be frittered away on inessential. It is also argued that the higher the propensity to consume the lesser will be the savings. This leads to problems of capital formation and so investment may be hindered. Supporters of this view ignore the fact that advertising has been use as a very potent tool for promoting banking services and savings habits and for raising funds from the public for investment in equity and debenture capital and fixed deposits. Over-subscription of a large number of capital issues in India in recent years is a testimony to effective and purposeful use of advertising.

Product Differentiation and Product Proliferation

Another factor affecting the firm's capacity to influence demand is product differentiation. In product-differentiation rests the opportunity for influencing consumers in developing brand preference. Products where differentiation is not possible will not be affected by advertising.

Advertising plays a part in expanding the range of merchandise through product differentiation. The desire on the part of producers to offer a variety of products under their brands has led them to continuing experimentation with different combinations of desirable product qualities. Technology has contributed in developing new products, which might gain consumers acceptance.

Critics of advertising point out that advertising encourages unnecessary product proliferation. It leads to multiplication of products that are almost identical resulting in wastage of resources, which would have been used to produce other products. It must be noted that artificial product differentiation based solely on advertising are fruitless as shown in the study by Lambin (1973). Rational economic considerations are probably a more important element in buying decisions than are widely assumed.

Catalyst for Innovation, Change and Quality

Advertising encourages product development by providing an economical way of informing potential buyers about the launch of new products or of the improvements in some products. In many situations, innovation requires large research and development expenditures and substantial investment in production facilities that might be difficult to justify if advertising could not be efficiently employed to communicate the existence of the innovation.

Creativity in advertising leads to the discovery of new relationships that change the prospect's perception. Two aspects of creativity are of special significance, the originality of the message communicated, and the eventual effect on consumers' standards of living. The ability to bring about changes comes from originality, ingenuity, innovation and imagination in advertising. This may be seen in upgrading of products/brands used by consumers. Greater aesthetic satisfaction from the use of better designed products resulting partly from advertising persuasion is another example of change.

Advertising not only tends to improve product quality through competition and product differentiation but it has some influence upon product quality in another way, that is inducing producers to maintain quality as claimed under their brand names. The system of branding is giving protection of the product quality to consumers, because the self-interest of sellers has led them to ensure a high quality of merchandise sold under their brands.

There could be advertising that is much better than the product. When that happens, all that the good advertising does is, put that business out of business faster. The most powerful element in advertising is the truth. A seller does not wish to maintain quality under his brand only because he is an advertiser. It is in his long-term interest to enjoy the benefits of patronage of satisfied customers, whether he advertises extensively or not.

Advertising and Competition

Advertising encourages competition and consequently firms vie with each other in providing the best products and services to buyers to create and sustain brand loyalty. This encourages firms to undertake research and offer products more suited to consumer needs.

It was found in a study by Lambin that a company's advertisement had a negative impact on rivals' sales/market shares. However, the study did not uncover any explosive pattern leading to advertising wars. Rival advertising efforts tend to cancel each other out.

There is a general belief that advertisements promote industrial concentration to a greater or lesser degree. The extent of such concentration may vary with the character of individual trade, the ability of the product to be advertised and the technical conditions of its production.

However, studies on this subject are not conclusive. The evidence of positive association between advertising and concentration is weaker than what can be expected.

Financial Support to Media & Democracy

The major functions of the mass media are to provide education, entertainment and information to the audience. The revenue from subscriptions alone is quite inadequate to support the publication of newspapers and magazines. Radio and television networks have to depend on the support of the state exchequer. Alternatively, they must have access to advertising revenue. Selling of space or time by the media to advertisers is essential for the financial viability of the media.

The acceptance of advertising enhances the potential for raising advertising revenues. This in turn helps the launching of new publications and expanding media in various ways.

This development is characteristic of the Indian media scene in recent years. A number of periodicals newspapers and satellite channels for TV transmission have been launched during the 90's.

Social and Ethical Issues in Advertising

Discussions on these issues usually covers both the means and effects of advertising. Means of advertising are attacked on grounds of deception, manipulation and bad taste. Some comments go to the extent of saying that *advertising may be described as the science of arresting the human intelligence long enough to get money from it.* Even Mark Twain had said, *"Many a small thing has been made large by the right kind of advertising."*

In the context of effect of advertising, its influence on social values and life styles are discussed. The all pervasiveness of advertising is believed to have impact on the value system of the society.

Deception

Deception occurs either when an advertisement is introduced into the perceptual process of the audience and the output of that perceptual process differs from the reality of the situation or effects buying behaviour to the detriment of the consumers. An ad can be deceptive in many aspects, including: (a) Price of a product (b) Quantity of a product (c) The quality or standard of the item (d)

Times, dates, and locations that the product is available (e) Information regarding warranties (f) False facts regarding deals or sales (g) Confusion over interest rates or other factors.

Thus, deception refers mainly to the information content in advertising but may also arise from misplaced emphasis in presentation. "There's an ad for every vice. That's advice."

H. G. Wells, a prolific English writer in many genres, including the novel, history, politics, and social commentary, and textbooks and rules for war games, a four times nominee for nobel prize in literature has a book by the title *The War in the Air: Advertising is legalized lying.*

The Supreme Court of the United States has laid down the following criteria for deceptive advertising:

a) Advertising must not observe or conceal material facts.

b) Advertising as a whole must not create a misleading impression although every statement separately considered is literally truthful.

c) Advertising must not be artfully continued to distract and direct readers' attention from the true nature of the terms and conditions of an offer.

d) Advertising must be free of fraudulent traps and strategy, which would induce action that would not result from a forthright disclosure of the true nature of the offer.

Manipulation

Critics of advertising feel that the freedom of choice, which consumers have, is restricted by the power of advertising since it can manipulate buyers into making a decision against their will or against their interests. If one wants to understand how a lion hunts, one must go to the jungle. Advertising brings a mirage of a jungle into the living rooms and make people believe that they are not in a zoo.

Such manipulation can occur by playing on subconscious motives of people using emotional or subliminal appeals. Even the genuine persuasive power of scientific advertising can have such effects. It must be pointed out that the manipulative capability of advertising through a careful application of techniques of motivation research has been vastly overstated.

People probably make choices most of the time for reasons best known to them. Although marketing professional have accepted the reduced scope of motivation research, the layman is still haunted by the spectre of the 'hidden persuaders'.

The communication of fact-based information about a product is usually accepted as being of value to the customer. However, when advertising utilises appeals or associations that go beyond such a basic communication task, the charge of manipulation via emotional appeals is raised. *"Advertising is the modern substitute for argument; its function is to make the worse appear the better."*

Taste

Some critics feel that advertising is objectionable because creative exposition may not always be in good taste. The most common criticisms are:

- a) Moral concern about the advertising related to the product itself, e.g. cigarettes, alcohol.

b) Objections to the occasion of exposure to the advertisement. This will be especially relevant to television advertising when children may be in the audience.

c) Objections to appeals employed, e.g. over emphasis on sex appeals.

d) Objections to the techniques of advertising strategy like excessive repetitions of the Claim or advertisement, or clearly displeasing presentation.

Materialism

Advertising is accused of promoting materialism among the public i.e. it induces people to attach too much importance to the material aspects of life. It creates the notion that acquisition of things will gratify basic and inner needs and aspirations.

As Mary Gardiner Jones, the PIC Commissioner has put it, "It is the message of the commercial that all of the major problems confronting an individual can be instantly eliminated by the application of some external force the use of a product.

Externally derived solutions are thus made the prescriptions for life's difficulties. All of our individual yearnings hopes and fears can yield instantly to a material solution and one which can work instantly without any effort, skill or trouble on our part."

Promoting Stereotypes

By portraying certain groups of individuals in certain roles, advertising promotes stereotypes. Women are usually, portrayed as homemakers or mothers. Brands do not think of themselves as storytellers but they are story builders. They plant seeds of content and let the community build on it by replicating and perpetuating stereotypes.

In a study done by IIM students (1980) it was found that in a majority of advertisements featuring woman along with other persons they are shown as mothers, wives or as companions to men, thus apparently relegating them to secondary role. Only in some cases are they shown as business executives.

Advertising to Children

People read and watch what interests them, and sometimes it is an ad. Can that be said for children as well? It is argued that children are more susceptible to deception. They lack the perceptual defences of adults, and that they cannot objectively evaluate advertisements. The real fact of the matter is that nobody reads ads. Thus, there is substantial scope for manipulation of children especially through television advertising.

In a study by Boddewyn (1980) for the International Advertising Association, it was noted that decency and sexism appeared to be less explosive issues than advertising to children.

Advertising and Sensitivity to Price

There is a belief that advertising affords differentiation among closely resembling brands and thus dulls the consumer's sensitivity to the prices. There is no significant difference between the various brands of whiskey, or cigarettes or beer. They are all about the same, so are the cake mixes and the detergents, and the margarines... The manufacturer who dedicates his advertising to building the most sharply defined personality for his brand gets the largest share of the market at the highest profit.

However, a study by Dick Wittink (1977) showed that the relative price elasticity increase as advertising share increases implying that advertising increases sensitivity to price.

Advertising Creates Insecurity

Advertising is accused of causing people to worry about tooth decay, body odour, lack of self-confidence and many other ills. The implication is that the advertiser claims that his product will induce these worries. Oscar Wilde advises, "Be yourself. Everyone else is already taken" but advertising says be like the endorsers and advocates of the brand.

The charge is true at least in part. There is no evidence that advertising can create a fear where no anxiety exists. However, it can magnify latent fears.

Advertising: An Engine for Welfare

Advertising is a potent vehicle for gaining the acceptance of desirable and useful concepts and ideas irrespective of the profit motive being minimal or missing altogether. This may be seen in the case of objectives like preventive aspects of public health, environment protection and renewal, developing the small family norm especially in overpopulated developing countries, dissuading child marriages, dowry or drunken driving, national integration, conservation of natural resources and so forth.

"*Certainly, it seems true enough that there's a good deal of irony in the world and it seemed true at the time I wrote the poem there was a good deal of deception also. I mean, if you live in a world full of politicians and advertising there's obviously a lot of deception. But I'm urging the reader in a somewhat over-simple way that despite the fact that he lives in such a time not to be hardened and spoiled by it."*

- Kenneth Koch (1993)

Debate about the social desirability of advertising has a long history and is characterized by very polarized positions. In the economics literature, there has been classical arguments stating how advertising may increase demand "by altering wants themselves". This is a manipulative form of advertising as it exploits "the laws of psychology" with which the consumer "is unfamiliar and, therefore, against which he cannot defend himself..." McFadden and Train (1996) define this as a form of persuasive advertising that changes consumer tastes or beliefs about the product without changing the actual product characteristics themselves.

Of course, not all forms of advertising are detrimental to society. Stigler (1961) and Telser (1964), 1964 contend that advertising can provide useful information, which leads consumers to lower priced products with more preferred characteristics.

In an earlier article Dixit and Norman (1978) studied the welfare effects of advertising. They came to the surprising conclusion that, even accepting post-advertising tastes as the welfare standard, monopoly advertising which raises price is excessive. The point of a comment by Carl Shapiro (1980) showed how and why their analysis failed to apply to the case where there is more than one consumer. Their analysis assumes that pre-advertising consumption is distributed efficiently according to post-advertising tastes. Since this is not generally the case, Shapiro showed that there are gains to advertising ignored by Dixit and Norman.

Stivers & Tremblay (2005) developed a model to show how advertising affects equilibrium prices, search costs, and social welfare in monopoly and imperfectly competitive markets. When informative advertising leads to a sufficient reduction in consumer search costs, both consumer and producer welfare may increase even though market prices rise. This conclusion has important implications for policy analysts, because it demonstrates that one cannot test the welfare effect of advertising by determining the impact of advertising on market prices alone. One must investigate the impact of advertising on both market prices and search costs to understand fully the welfare effect of advertising.

That advertising has the capabilities and strengths to shape and mould public opinion is more than established, but the instances of misuses of this strength like the misuse of any other political, social or religious power are also quite visible.

It is the judicious application of this power like all others for the common good of masses, which is the need of the hour.

2

Glitches & Hitches in Gauging Success of Advertising

Business invests many billions of dollars in advertising each year. Those companies that advertise most persistently are very likely to spend more on advertising in a year than they achieve in net income. Guttmann (2019) reported that the spending on advertising worldwide has been increasing steadily and is expected to surpass 560 billion U.S. dollars in 2019. North America is the region that invests most in the sector, followed by Asia and Western Europe. Middle East and Africa as well as Central and Eastern Europe spend the least. The largest ad market in the world, the United States, invested more than 229 billion U.S. dollars in advertising in 2018, while China, second in the ranking, invested less than half of the amount in the same period. American consumer goods corporation Procter & Gamble was the largest advertiser worldwide in 2017, having spent more than 10 billion U.S. dollars on ads. Other big advertisers include Dutch-British Unilever, French L'Oréal, and German Volkswagen, respectively second, third and fourth in the ranking.

The COVID-19 pandemic has caused a contraction in 2020, which is being seen as an unforeseen and temporary event. Guttmann (2020), revising her earlier estimates reported that advertising spending worldwide will fall to 517 billion U.S. dollars in 2020, representing a decline of roughly 11.8 percent compared with the previous year.

The executives approving advertising budgets are almost unanimous in their belief that advertising is an efficient marketing tool relative to available alternatives. Thus, it may be said that the business community is in accord about the usefulness and effectiveness of advertising.

Advertising Works

The critics of advertising are certain about its effectiveness. It is, from their viewpoint, so effective that it can make people do what the advertiser wants them to do, whether they wish to do it or not and even if it is not in their best interest. Critics of advertising are so certain of advertising's power that they believe it must be limited through government regulation or advertiser self-restraint if consumers are to be adequately protected from it.

Advertisements are produced in tens of thousands daily, throughout the year and throughout the world. The advertising practitioner, in the creation of advertisements, moves through a more or less determined and common series of professional steps. Inherent in these professional steps is the belief that if they are followed, the resulting advertisements will be effective in increasing the probability that those consumers who are exposed to them will behave or think as the advertiser wishes them to do. The practitioners have enough sense of professionalism and pride in craft to believe that every advertisement they produce has a strong chance to produce such a positive effect. They do not believe that they are engaged in a game of chance or in an activity that is only occasionally or randomly successful.

Jerry W. Thomas, President/CEO of Dallas-Fort Worth based Decision Analyst in a whitepaper in 2020 says, "The advertising industry, as a whole, has the poorest quality-assurance systems and turns out the most inconsistent product (their ads and commercials) of any industry in the world. This might seem like an overly harsh assessment, but it is based on testing thousands of ads over several decades. In our experience, only about half of all commercials actually work; that is, have any positive effects on consumers' purchasing behaviour or brand choice. Moreover, a small share of ads actually appear to have negative effects on sales. How could these assertions possibly be true? Don't advertising agencies want to produce great ads? Don't clients want great advertising? Yes, yes, they do, but they face formidable barriers"

Decision Analyst is a research and analytical consulting firm serving major corporations, advertising agencies, and marketing consultancies in the Americas, Europe, Asia, the Middle East, and Africa.

Thomas lists creative ego, ignorance and speculative beliefs as major barriers to effective advertising. He adds that agencies and clients have a mistaken belief that they know how to create and judge good advertising, and there is no need for advertising testing. The belief that sales performance alone can reveal if the advertising is working undermines, and thwart efforts to objectively pre-test advertising. Clients suffer from lack of strategy, or having a poor strategy and agencies hide behind their ineptness.

Effects of Advertising

Yet, in spite of all of this, it is true that no one knows exactly what effects advertising causes or how these effects are caused. Advertising practitioners are hard put to tell why some advertisements are more effective or seem to be more effective than other advertisements. Even if some specialist advertisers (direct response and retail) can predict a level of sales response from a particular advertisement or advertising expenditure, based upon experience or experimentation, they do not know what the advertising did to those consumers who were moved by it, or why it did not move those consumers who were equally ready to purchase but yet did not. Some general advertisers may be able to predict a national level of market response on the basis of test market experience for specific products and market experience for specific products and specific advertising programs, but no general advertisers are able to predict what a particular advertising programme will produce unless they have accumulated much past experience to serve as a basis for such a prediction. And even if experience or testing in some instances, may provide a basis for predicting market response to advertising campaigns, they do not give a basis for assessing the potential of particular individual advertisements.

Mechanism of Advertising Effects

Almost no one who is involved with advertising doubts that it works. Yet, almost no one who is involved with advertising can specify the exact effects that an advertisement causes to produce change in its audience's behaviour, knowledge, or attitude. Nor is it possible, therefore, to describe exactly how advertising causes sales. As Philip Nelson (1974) expresses it, *"We all know that advertising increases the sales of those who advertise, but that knowledge does not get us very far ... it is necessary to specify how advertising increases sales to be able to say very much about advertising."*

It is not unusual in human events for one to know that some activity causes a specific result while being unable to describe the exact mechanisms or processes that produce this result.

Aeronautical engineers must depend upon wind tunnels to forecast the performance of airplane wings, and pharmaceutical companies must test experimental drug products with animals before attempting to use them with humans. There is at least as much trial and error in most human enterprises as there is tested and fool-proof theory, and advertising is surely not an exception.

But just as perfected theory helps design heavier air frames today than 20 years ago and more effective prescription drugs today than 40 years ago, so also it is hoped and expected that more sophisticated theory in advertising will, in due course, lead to more effective advertising at lower cost and with less waste.

This chapter sets out some of the current theoretical thoughts about the process of advertising. The objective is to suggest the general direction of contemporary thought, not to explain alternative theories in detail or to select a particular preferred theory.

Theoretical Developments

There will be a gradual improvement in our understanding of how advertising works as the development of theory proceeds on several different fronts and under a variety of different assumptions. Progress in the development of advertising theory has not, however, been as rapid as one might wish, and, as a pioneer advertising researcher Darrell suggested in 1974, progress in the future may continue at a surprisingly slow pace. He says, *"Forty years ago, when advertising measures were just developing and after books on advertising theory had become commonplace, it seemed realistic to expect that the American bicentennial would find advertising practice solidly based on accepted theory and that advertising research would be practiced by academically trained professionals equipped with widely accepted and validated techniques of measurement. To achieve this stature by 1976, the advertising industry and its academic counterpart will have to hurry."*

Basic Assumptions of Professionals

At this point, it will be valuable to summarize the major assumptions that advertising practitioners make as they practice advertising in the last decade of this century. Such a summary provides background and a reference point against which to evaluate theoretical viewpoints to consider whether any of these theoretical viewpoints are inconsistent with current advertising practice. It will also help assess whether certain theoretical viewpoints, if generally accepted in the future, will affect contemporary advertising practice in any significant way.

The following paragraphs summarize the assumptions of advertising practitioners.

    1   ***Advertising Is Communication***. The purpose of advertising is to communicate information - logical emotional, or evaluative - to prospective purchasers or to people who will affect the advertiser's future goals in one way or another.

    2   ***Advertising Communication Convinces*** its recipients and predisposes them to act. This action will occur either immediately, or at some time in the future.

    3   ***The Basis of Effective Advertising Communication is Two Fold***:

    a)   First, effective advertising communication is based on comprehensive knowledge about potential advertising recipients.

    b)   Nevertheless, in addition, effective advertising communication requires significant ski, or even genius, to assure the information communicated about a product or corporation will increase the probability that consumers will think or do what the advertiser wants them to think or do.

4   *Advertising Effects Are Accomplished Over Time.* Consumers are not continuously in the market for advertised products. When consumers do come into the market to make a purchase, they frequently purchase a brand toward which they are loyal, or a brand that is available, or a brand with an attractive package, or a brand with a lower price, rather than some of the brands for which they have attended to advertising.

5   Similarly, when a particular institution becomes important to consumers not only in terms of their advertising assertions, but also in terms of their advertising weight; the perceived meaningfulness of advertising messages interacts with the gross number of messages the consumer experiences for the advertised product, service, or institution. ***Effective advertising says something important to consumers*** and says it as many times as the advertiser can afford.

6   *Advertising Effect Is Cumulative.* Advertising effect builds over time. As facts that are important to consumers are delivered to them, they gradually become more likely to respond favourably to those brands or companies whose advertising seems to them to be most meaningful.

7   *Advertising Affects Brand or Company Momentum.* The advertising program maintains brand or company momentum; and outstanding advertising program accelerates brand or company momentum; declining brand or company momentum reflects a substandard advertising program. The

cumulative effect of each advertising program depends upon its immediate effect. These assumptions permit the modern practice of copy testing, which focuses upon the immediate reaction of consumers to advertising copy.

8   Problems of Consumer Complexity. It is one thing to speculate about how advertising works in the process of marketing, and another to assess the effects of advertising upon consumers. Except perhaps for retail advertisements, consumers have no particular reason to attend to advertisements; they certainly do not set out each day with the objective of absorbing advertising messages. Although it is wrong to assume that consumers will assiduously attend non-retail advertising. It is equally erroneous to assume that its exhortations will be slavishly followed; it is by no means clear, how the assertions of such advertising become intertwined in consumer's lives.

9   The Advertising Practitioner Works with Imperfect Knowledge.

Advertising practitioners learn as much as they can about the consumer, try to be as creative in developing messages as they can, give the job of making advertisements their best and then hope for the best. Even if practitioners think they know exactly what they are doing as they go through their 'we-articulated' professional steps of creating advertisements, they and their work are ultimately at the mercy of the consumer and the way in which consumers perceive and process the advertising stimuli that they receive. It is the fact that it is difficult to know how advertising messages are absorbed by the consumer that makes the prediction of advertising effects so difficult.

Excellence-Perplexity Fringe in Advertising

It should be clear by now that the world we see, hear, feel, touch and smell is not related in a simple manner to the world described by the physicist. If a simple transformation of the physical world could allow predicting what a person perceives, it would not be necessary for the science of psychology to exist. In such a situation, the organism could be viewed as an instrument to blur the image of the world. One could compensate for this blurring effect and pretend that the organism does not exist at all.

Despite the convenience of this point of view, however, it is an unfortunate fact that stimulation of the organism results in perceptions that cannot be predicted from the stimulus itself. The organism transforms the signals it receives in a complicated manner.

It is at just this point -- at the interface between professional excellence and professional perplexity- that the need arises for an articulated theory of the way in which consumers and advertising interact. The hope is that over time theory will develop that will have implications on both sides of the interface, improving professional excellence as it diminishes professional perplexity.

In-depth interviews with senior-level agency practitioners (creative, planning, and account directors) were conducted to explore their thoughts about how advertising works. The study was designed to add to the understanding of the academician-practitioner gap in advertising by uncovering practitioners' hypothesized knowledge autonomy in the context of the sociological theory of professionalization. Results provide evidence for the existence of such autonomous practitioner knowledge schemas. Agency practitioners' core theories include a two-step "break through and engage" process and the longitudinal "mutation of effects" idea. They also believe in the primacy of emotional effects. Creativity is identified as the singularly most important factor in effectiveness, and agency professionals resisted any other regularities that may curtail creativity and result in formulaic advertising. Practitioners also emphasized the importance of defining boundary conditions when making claims about how advertising works, and identified strategic campaign objective, product category, medium used, and historical time period as key domains to consider.

David Ogilvy had said, *"I don't know the rules of grammar. If you're trying to persuade people to do something, or buy something, it seems to me you should use their language."*

Of course, the practitioners do not stop doing advertising work simply because they have no adequate theory to make sure that every advertisement they develop will be effective.

"The best ideas come as jokes. Make your thinking as funny as possible," Ogilvy had propounded.

Probably most practitioners are not even aware that they would do better advertising if they had a perfect theory of how advertising accomplishes its effects. Practitioners continue to make advertisements, following the basic assumption about their craft that promise to deliver advertising at a high level of professional competence, and leave worries about theory in advertising to others.

These "others" tend to be advertising researchers, both academic and professional, who recognise the weaknesses in copy testing procedures that do not predict market response and the inefficiencies in market tests that develop narrow generalizations at best, only after many individual tests.

It is true that as of late 2020, there is no single theory upon which all can agree about how advertising produces its effects. There is instead, a variety of competitive theories.

Some of these theories offer alternative explanations of the same phenomena, whereas others may offer complementary explanations of different but ill-defined phenomena. In considering an advertising theory, one must assess not only its explanation of how advertising causes its effects, but also its generality as an explanation of the advertising process.

How Advertising Works: Status of Theory

It appears possible to divide the main current, theoretical formulations of the advertising process into four groupings. These four theoretical divisions are the pressure-response theories; the active learning theories; the low-involvement theories; and the dissonance reduction theories.

Pressure - Response Theories of Advertising

One group of theories about how advertising works emphasizes advertising pressure or weight as the cause of advertising effect. Such theories depend upon the determination of a relation between dollars spent upon advertising or advertising messages delivered to consumers and sales response to those dollars spent or messages delivered. The exact form of the relationship may be developed deductively from the study of relationships between advertising and product sales over a time. Alternatively, the form of relationship may be developed inductively, usually based upon the use of response functions transferred from some other discipline, such as psychology or physics.

The economist Philip Nelson, for example, has postulated that advertising for relatively low value, frequently, purchased "experience goods" is effective in the degree to which the consumer perceives the advertiser to be light or heavy advertiser. Nelson suggests that the more messages about a product or brand a consumer perceives; the more likely the consumer is to be affected by that advertising.

As Nelson puts it: *"The purpose of the advertising for experience goods is to convince the consumer that the brand is a heavy advertiser. The more advertising messages of which the consumer is aware, the more likely he is to try the brand."*

Many management scientists have developed analytical models, which depend upon advertising response functions that have been deduced from the study of advertising sales relationships. These functions tend to vary from product class to product class and may also vary from geographic region to geographic region, from season to season, and from brand to brand within product category.

For example, Ambar Rao and Peter G. Miller (1975) have described a procedure for empirically estimating advertising to sales relations from historical data. The procedure has two steps:

    a) *The derivation of empirical advertising response coefficients for the brand under study for each of a number of sales districts.*

    b) *The synthesis of the empirical advertising response coefficients into a general model of sales response to advertising...*

The procedure has been tested using data from a number of brands of consumer-packaged goods. In every case, the sales to advertising relationship were successfully estimated.

The Anheuser-Busch studies of Russell Ackoff and his colleagues are good examples of the inductive approach to the formulation of advertising theory.

As Ackoff and Emshoff (1975) put it:
"*Since we knew of no tested theory, we fabricated our own. Our hunch was that advertising could be considered to be a stimulus and sales a response to it. Much is known about the general nature of stimulus-response functions."*

In this instance, the sales response to advertising function was developed upon the basis of prior studies of the stimulus-response function in psychology. Two general response function shapes are described in the pressure-response theory literature.

One, perhaps most frequently discussed, is the so called "S" curve: This is the curve that Rao and Miller describe, and it is the curve used by Ackoff in the Anheuser-Busch studies. Proponents of the "S" curve maintain that advertising spending is less efficient below certain threshold levels and that a critical mass of advertising weight is necessary for marketers to obtain optimal returns from advertising.

A second class of curve is discussed. It represents continuously decreasing sales returns to advertising inputs. In this formulation, the first advertisement is always more productive than its successors. According to this view, each successive dollar spent for advertising yields less than the former one in terms of sales revenues generated.

Simon and Arndt (1980) made a comprehensive review of the evidence regarding these two curve forms and concluded that the S-curve and its increasing returns to adverting are not supported by evidence:

"... the near unanimity of these very different sorts of studies is impressive. If there were increasing returns, some of these studies should show it."

Simon and Arndt did not include all of the pertinent studies in their review. (There is no citation, for example, of Ackoff's Anheuser-Busch work.) Some proprietary studies, as reported by Jones (1983) in addition, do confirm the existence of the S-shaped sales response function particularly for the case of packaged goods advertising.

But setting aside controversy about the shape of the sales response curves, the pressure response theories of advertising insist that advertising pressure causes sales, and that it is, a single factor that can be related to sales results.

Leo Bogart (1978) makes the point:

"In econometric studies of advertising, it appears to be tacitly assumed by both critics and supporters that creative quality must be considered a constant. Its variability is as summed to be random and to fall within about the same range that could be expected in product performance or in entrepreneurial talent from firm to firm. This assumption is critical and also mistaken."

Pressure-response theories have been criticized for two principal reasons:
      a) Not all advertising sales relations maintain relative stability over a period of time or from geographic area to area. The

problem is not that sales response relations can not be deduced from a study of sales and advertising data. Rather, the problem is that the revealed relationships vary in time and by geographic region to such an extent that they may not seem stable enough for precise advertising appropriation determination. Or, to put it another way, they may not be stable enough to change established methods of appropriation determination in many companies.

b) Pressure-response theories totally ignore the creative function in advertising. That is, these theories imply that any advertising message at all will do, as long as it is repeated a sufficient number of times. This presumption offends almost all practitioners of advertising, because they have come to believe, on the basis of their experience, that message content does matter and that variations in message strength will be reflected in variations in sales.

There is evidence that the experience of advertising practitioners is correct; sales do go up when particularly effective advertising messages are introduced, and sales do fade when weaker advertising messages are run. Beyond this, the notion that the consumer is a kind of anvil that responds in direct proportion to the number of times advertising strikes, seems to contradict the growing understanding of the way in which consumers process information, including advertising.

"A good ad should be like a good sermon: It must not only comfort the afflicted, it also must afflict the comfortable" said Bernice Bowles Fitz-Gibbon (1894-1982) an American advertising woman, inducted into the Advertising Hall of Fame in 1982.

If pressure-response theories in pure form turn out to be amenable to a refinement beyond that which now seems possible and ultimately come to predict generally precise and stable relations between sales and advertising weight, the practice of advertising will change radically. Lesser emphasis would then be necessary upon creativity and the nature and quality of the creative product. Copy testing would become very irrelevant. Finally, much more emphasis would presumably be placed upon media planning and the fine-tuning of message delivery procedures.

Active Learning Theories in Advertising

The active learning theories of advertising assume that advertising conveys information to consumers that may be sufficiently meaningful to them to change their attitude toward the advertised brand. Favourable attitude change increases predisposition of the consumer to purchase or probability of consumer purchase; the more the increase in favourable attitude, the greater the probability of increased purchase and the greater the sales response. This is, of course, a general statement of the hierarchy-of-effects model, and it is an accurate reflection of the assumptions held by most practitioners about how advertising works.

The important aspect of these active learning theories is that they all contain at least three elements; information that is learned; attitudes that are changed because of learning; and behaviour that responds to attitude change. All these models specify the exact sequence of events that lead to advertising response; learning → attitude change → behaviour change.

Alvin Achenbaum (1972) describes the process upon which active learning theories of advertising are based: "*Information about one or more product attributes which are salient to consumers is communicated in a persuasive context by national advertising. These attributes can be sensory, evaluative, or emotional. If the communication is persuasive enough to improve consumer attitudes on that attribute, their attitudes toward the overall brand will improve as we. This improvement in overall brand attitudes will concomitantly increase the probability of purchase."*

The earlier formulations of this theory tended to assume that the consumer is in constant search for information improve or confirm all purchase decisions and that advertising is one of the kinds of information that the consumer has available in this ongoing process.

"A good advertisement is one which sells the product without drawing attention to itself. In the modern world of business, it is useless to be a creative, original thinker unless you can also sell what you create."

Donald Cox (1969) identified three sources of consumer information,

(i) *marketer-dominated channels of communication*, including the product, its advertising, its package, its promotion, its distribution, its shelf display, and personal selling;

(ii) *consumer-dominated channels of communication*, including all inter personal sources of information-word of mouth-not under control of the marketer; and

(iii) *neutral information sources* that are influenced by neither the marketer nor the consumer, such as Consumer Reports, product appraisals by such consumer advocated as Ralph Nader and others.

Deluged with information, the consumer is constantly faced with the problem of sorting out that, which is meaningful to him and adequate to his purpose.

In Cox's formulation, consumers were likely to settle for information from marketer-dominated, or formal, channels, if consumers believe they have relatively little to lose in psychic or economic terms.

If the risk of loss is perceived to be higher the consumer might actively look for information of a higher grade and/or reliability such as that available from the consumer (informal) channels or neutral sources. Cox summarizes the argument:

"I have argued that consumers tend to use information channels that is, consumer-dominated and neutral sources primarily in those situations in which perceived risk and uncertainty have not been sufficiently reduced by formal information sources and where risk uncertainty, and involvement are high enough to justify seeking information through informal channels."

In recent years, the formulation of learning theories of advertising that is reflected in the Cox approach has been modified by the notion that consumers' actual involvement with the purchase decisions is not always high.

Thus, the more contemporary view is that there are many kinds of purchase decisions that involve relatively little risk for the consumer.

For consumer purchase decisions of low involvement, the adult consumer rarely seeks information actively, and other formulations of 'how advertising works' may be more apt. Nevertheless, for those purchase decisions that involve high risk in Cox's terms or, perhaps, search goods in Nelson's formulation, there is active learning theory seems highly relevant.

Michael Ray describes the conditions under which active consumer information seeking and the learning→attitude change→purchase behavior change - theory seems most appropriate. Research by Maguire and others seems to indicate that it typically occurs when the audience is involved in the topic of the campaign and when there are clear differences between alternatives.

Research on diffusion of new products and innovation provides the best illustration of such conditions. Those audiences that are most interested in new ideas are involved, and new products or ideas offer clear alternatives. It is under such conditions that audience members first become aware, then develop interest, make evaluations, try, and adopt - the 'adoption process hierarchy'.

In recent years, the literature of advertising has contained many references to "consumer information processing." This approach is concerned with studying just how consumers acquire and process information so that it ultimately affects their behaviour. The consumer information processing approach is in effect, a general formulation of the active learning or hierarchical theories of advertising, and, as such, has both the strengths and weaknesses of such theories. There are many great technicians in advertising. Moreover, unfortunately, they talk the best game. They know all the rules ... but there is one little rub. They forget that advertising is persuasion, and persuasion is not a science, but an art. Advertising is the art of persuasion.

As William McGuire (1978) defines it: *"The information-processing approach to social influence posits a series of behavioural steps through which the individual must pass if he is effectively to be persuaded."*

Active learning theories of advertising are generally criticised on the basis that they do not explain all consumer-advertising interactions. The critics of the active learning formulations do not believe that these formulations do not believe that these formulations identify the wrong elements in the process of consumer advertising interaction; they agree that learning, attitude change, and behaviour change are the relevant variables to explain consumer-advertising interaction. Rather, the critics are more concerned with the sequence that is postulated by active learning theories; that is, they do not agree that learning always pre cedes attitude change and that attitude change always precedes behaviour change. The exact meaning of these criticisms will become clear in the following discussion of low-involvement and dissonance theories of advertising.

Even as the active learning theories are criticised, it is important to recognize that they are in close congruence with the assumptions that the advertising practitioner holds as he goes about his daily practice of advertising. To simplify the nine assumptions held by the advertising practitioner and presented earlier in this chapter, we could say that he believes pertinent information must be communicated to change attitudes to cause sales. Incorporating the pressure-response theories, he believes that the more often one communicates pertinent information, the more dramatically will attitude change and behaviour change occur in favour of the advertised brand.

In spite of current criticism, if one were to believe that active learning theories of advertising thoroughly explain all consumer advertising interaction, very little change in the assumptions of practitioners would result. This formulation is in closest accord with their current conceptions.

It is also important to point out that most of contemporary copy testing practice is based upon active learning theories of advertising. Most, if not all, of the recall methods and most, if not all, of the attitude change methods reflect this formulation.

Low-Involvement Theories of Advertising

The critics of active learning theories of advertising believe that much consumer-advertising interaction involves low consumer involvement and a lack of active information seeking. In this view, the consumer without conscious search, appraisal, or resistance absorbs a great deal of advertising information.

The advertising is neither evaluated nor processed into new or revised attitudes; it simply goes into storage.

When the same message is repeatedly stored in this way, it may cause a change in the consumer's awareness of the brand and/or the mental weight accorded to it. This change in brand awareness or salience may ultimately lead to the possibility of purchase, even though there has been, in this process, no overt change in the attitude the consumer holds about the brand.

After purchase and use, attitude may change, but it will change because of brand experience rather than as a direct result of advertising effect. The low-involvement formulation involves the same elements as the active learning theory learning, attitude change, and behaviour change.

However, the sequence of these elements as advertising and consumers interact is postulated to be different.

In the low-involvement formulation, it is theorized that learning occurs first, followed by behaviour change and, finally, changed behaviour causes a subsequent change in attitude.

Thus, the low-involvement formulation involves a hierarchy of effects, but it is a different hierarchy than in active learning formulations. The low-involvement hierarchy is learning → behavior-change → attitude-change.

Michael Ray suggests that low involvement consumer-advertising interactions do not occur universally, but in particular kinds of brand environments: *"The Low Involvement hierarchy most often occurs when there are minimal differences between alternatives or when low involvement makes actual differences unimportant to the audience."*

The distinction between high and low involvement consumer-advertising interactions was apparently first made by Herbert E. Krugman as he studied interactions between consumers and the television medium.

In a classic paper published in 1965, he postulated that television communication was unique: *"I have tried to say that the public lets down its guard to the repetitive commercial use of the television medium and that it easily changes its ways of perceiving products and brands and its purchasing behaviour without thinking very much about it at the time of TV exposure or at any time prior to purchase; and without up to then changing verbalized attitudes… The significance of conditions of high or low involvement is not that one is better than the other, but that the processes of communication impact are different. That is, there is a difference in the change processes that are at work. Thus with low involvement, one might look for gradual shifts in perceptual structure, aided by repetition activated by behavioural choice situations, and followed at some time by attitude change."*

Later, Krugman (1971) measured brain waves of a single subject as she watched three television commercials, which seemed overtly to vary significantly in their visual impact. He was surprised to discover relatively little variation in brain wave patterns from commercial to commercial. Rather, his data indicated a basic mode of brain response to the television medium, unrelated to the specific content conveyed by the medium at a particular point in time.

"The subject was no more trying to learn something from television than she would be trying to learn something from a park landscape while resting on a park bench...

What shall we say of it, a communication medium that may effortlessly transmit into storage high quantities of information not thought about at the time of exposure, but much of it capable of later activation?"

Krugman's crucial insight is that learning may affect behaviour without the intermediate necessity of affecting attitudes. This concept is very consistent with the idea that most brand decisions among frequently purchased convenience goods are trivial and not tied strongly to closely held consumer value or belief systems. Consumers do not seem to seek information in many product categories actively.

No matter how important the brands within these product categories may be to their manufacturers and advertising agencies, the consumer does not consider them important. Thus, the consumer is not likely to seek out information about such products or to keep up to information about such products or to keep up to date about claims and counterclaims made by the advertisers in the category, and yet, this does not mean that advertising is not important to these categories.

It means, rather, that advertising messages are processed passively rather than actively and that the advertising effects cannot be traced through the rational chain of overt learning effects.

Andrew Ehrenberg has studied consumer purchase behaviour over a broad range of products. In a theoretical description of such behaviour that he calls the A-T-R model (Awareness-Trial- Reinforcement), Ehrenberg has emphasized the importance of advertising in reinforcing initial brand purchase decisions to produce repeat purchases of the same brand. He emphasizes repeat purchase behaviour, and advertising's effect upon it, because so large a portion of every brand's sales volume is made up of repeat purchases by a group of consumers who remain more or less loyal to the brand. Ehrenberg (1974) describes the process as follows:

"... consumers first gain awareness or interest in a product. Next they may make a trial purchase. Finally a repeat buying habit may be developed and reinforced if there is satisfaction after previous usage."

Ehrenberg's approach is distinctive in its emphasis upon repeated purchases and the importance of advertising in reinforcing repeat purchase behaviour.

The Ehrenberg A-T-R model appears to have the same basis as the low involvement theories of advertising. It suggests that attitude change follows behaviour change; in the terminology used above. Ehrenberg's

"Awareness" in not unlike Learning; his "Trial" is not unlike Behaviour; and his "Reinforcement" is not unlike Attitude Change.

Low involvement theories of advertising, as currently formulated, seem to have two characteristics. First, they seem especially applicable to television, especially because of the way in which Krugman has developed his own thought in conjunction with television and its effects. But, second, the low involvement theories seem especially we-suited to those non-television advertisements with minimal hard information content. The performance of advertisements that emphasize the brand name in an embellished context, but convey almost no additional information about the brand or its performance characteristics, may be better explained by low involvement theories of how advertising works than by active learning theories. For example, the effect of much cigarette advertising may be best understood through the low involvement. This has two implications:

a) One wonders if variations in involvement are a function solely of product categories. Most of the literature on the subject seems to take for granted that the purchase of some products involves high interest and/or high potential risks for the consumer and that it is this quality that determines the degree of involvement that will characterize the subsequent consumer advertising interaction.

But, is it not possible that involvement potential may vary among individuals? The suggestion is that individuals vary widely in their interest in product categories and in the degree of risk they perceive in purchase within particular product categories. If this is so, is it not likely that individual involvement levels may interact with product category differences in determining the degree of involvement an individual may evidence relative to particular advertising?

b) One also wonders there is a continuum of consumer involvement among product categories. As the literature now stands, involvement for a particular product category is a rather cut-and-dried concept; consumer product interaction is either high in involvement or it is not.

Now, we would have to classify the low-involvement theories of advertising as promising but not fully developed. Until the notions of variations in consumer involvement potential and variations in product-category-involvement potential have been refined, it is difficult to predict the ultimate impact of low-involvement theories.

If one were to speculate about how the practice of advertising might adapt itself to a widespread acceptance of low- involvement theories, for at least some product categories, he would make three observations:

a) *Acceptance of the low-involvement theories would call into question copy research procedures based upon recall of advertised messages. The point at issues is that under low-involvement theories it seems to make little difference what the consumer learns we enough to recall as a result of his exposure to an advertising message. The consumer is not really expected to learn very much information from advertising; rather, it is expected that he will passively absorb the fact that products are advertised. This absorption process will continue over a period of time until the nature of brand presence in the consumer's cognitive structure gradually changes, becoming in the process more salient to him.*

Thomas S. Robertson (1960) carries the idea to its logical conclusion. "Most advertising research assumes that a message gets through if it achieves recall on a short-term basis. This is the operational measure on which most advertising research funds are expended and on which most campaign decisions are based. If this is what we mean by message reception, then most messages do not get through. But, what if a message gains consumer exposure, although not short-term recall? Could not exposures alone be a sufficient cause of effects under conditions of low-commitment consumer behaviour when the amount of learning necessary is often totally minimal? We would then argue that exposure may correlate highly with impact under low-commitment conditions."

Under this conception, the, recall measures of at least some advertising, for example, advertising that is not created to satisfy the information needs of highly involved consumers, would be outmoded. Emphasis of research would shift for these product categories to the measurement of consumer exposure to advertising, and perhaps measures of changes in the awareness and salience of the advertised entity. The practitioner would be less concerned with transmitting specific, detailed information about the advertised entity than perhaps in communicating a generalized, positive picture of his product, service, or institution as frequently as possible.

> b) Acceptance of low-involvement theories would call into question copy research procedures that measure attitude change induced by exposure to advertising messages. There has been a considerable amount of research in recent years on the question of the relation between attitude and attitude change on the one hand and behaviour and behaviour change on the other. There has been in general, a disturbing lack of correlation between attitude change and subsequent behaviour change.

The low-involvement interpretation of this phenomenon is that attitude changes do not predict behaviour because they occur after behaviour and thus are formed only after, and because of behaviour. Whatever else such an interpretation would mean for the practice of advertising, it would certainly reduce enthusiasm for attitude change measures of advertising effect, at least in those product categories acknowledged to be characterized by low-involvement response to advertising.

> c) *Finally, it seems likely that acceptance of low-involvement theories of advertising might not have too much effect on the practitioners' firmly held belief that it is their job to convey, in advertising, positive information about products to consumers. For what, after all, does advertising convey to consumers except some sort of positive information about products?*

An acceptance of the low-involvement formulation might lead to revisions in current practice as to the amount of specific information that is necessary to convey to consumers about products.

One might be inclined to sacrifice message length and the relatively detailed copy messages that it implies for shorter more frequent messages and the greater opportunity for more frequent advertising exposure.

All of this is nothing more than speculation. The advertising industry will learn more about the whole concept of involvement in the years ahead. The idea of low and high involvement products is obsolete already. The new thinking is that buyers have involvement with the context of buying, including the purpose of buying, the economic, temporal and psychological resources available and the perceived risks in the eventuality of the buying decision turning out to be sub-optimal or wrong.

Dissonance Reduction Theories of Advertising

The final classification of theories of advertising involves the concept of cognitive dissonance originally formulated by Leon Festinger, and since developed in its implications for advertising by several others.

Cognitive dissonance occurs when a person perceives or experiences something that departs from his sense of reality. When the person perceives or experiences a distortion from his perception of what is "normal" or "real", cognitive dissonance results. His perception of normality or reality will then tend to force the dissonant perception or experience to influence his conception of what is real or normal. Festinger (1957) explains the initial phenomenon as follows:

> "... elements of cognition correspond for the most part with what the person actually does or feels or with what actually exists in the environment. In the case of opinions, beliefs, and values, the reality may be what is encountered experientially or what others have told him.
> But let us here object and say that persons frequently have cognitive elements which deviate markedly from reality, at least as we see it. Consequently, the major point to be made is that the reality which impinges on a person will exert pressures in the direction of bringing the appropriate cognitive elements into correspondence with that reality."

What, one may ask, does all of this have to do with advertising and consumer interactions with advertising? The answer is that when a consumer experiences dissonance, he may change his attitude structure in order to reduce the dissonance. Consumers may find, as their attitudes change, that they seek information in advertising that will help to explain, or justify, their newly formed attitudes.

This would differ from low-commitment behaviour because active search for information is involved, and this is incompatible with low-commitment behaviour. It differs from the active learning formulation because behaviour is the first step in the dissonance hierarchy.

When dissonance is present, some behaviour, it is postulated, has already occurred to produce dissonance, and it is this behaviour-caused dissonance that leads to subsequent restructuring of attitude. When dissonance is reduced through attitude change, information is sought to reinforce the change in attitude. In this formulation, the familiar elements of learning, attitude change, and behaviour change are present once again, but in another sequence. The sequence this time is behaviour change→ attitude change→ learning change (with consequent reduction of behaviour-induced dissonance). Michael Ray had described this sequence, calling it the dissonance-attribution hierarchy:

"The consumer or pseudo-consumer is forced to make a choice of behaviour on the basis of some non-media or non-marketing communication source. Thus he or she changes attitude in order to bolster that choice-offer on the basis of experience with the chosen alternative. Finally, learning itself occurs on a selective basis. In order to bolster the original choice by response to messages that are supportive of it."

There is little enough in the advertising literature about this particular formulation beyond its statement.

One reason for this is that in this theory, advertising is assigned a passive role in the causation of behaviour. Behaviour occurs, attitudes change, and advertising then enters the picture, supplying information as a kind of rationalizing and stabilizing force.

This point of view, of course, will find little support among the majority holding the view that advertising cause behavior, however this causal effect is achieved.

Therefore, for the moments, dissonance reduction theories are more or less in limbo. They may explain some consumer-advertising interactions, but in the absence of evidence to the contrary, it is probably safe to assume that only a small fraction of these interactions follow the dissonance reduction formulation.

Advertising Theory: Some Possibilities

The above review of theory in advertising suggests that there is no consensus about how consumers interact with advertising and how these specific interactions do or do not lead to particular results in the market place.

Leaving aside the pressure response theories of advertising because they are essentially unconcerned with the nature of consumer processing and use of advertising information, attention can be drawn to those theories that involve the elements of

    a) Learning
    b) Attitude change, and
    c) Behaviour change.

These three elements can take six separate sequences:

Sequence 1, 2, 3:   Learning→ Attitude Change→ Behaviour Change
                    (Active Learning)
Sequence 1, 3, 2:   Learning→ Behaviour Change→ Attitude Change
                    (Low Involvement)
Sequence 2, 1, 3:   Attitude Change→ Learning→ Behaviour Change
Sequence 2, 3, 1:   Attitude Change→ Behaviour Change→ learning
Sequence 3, 1, 2:   Behaviour Change→ Learning→ Attitude Change
Sequence 3, 2, 1:   Behaviour Change→ Attitude Change→ Learning
                    (Dissonance Reduction)

The preceding discussion has brought forth only three of these sequences,
> Sequence 1 → → 2 → → 3;
> Sequence 1 → → 3 → → 2; and
> Sequence 3 → → 2 → → 1.

One reason for this could be that the current-status of theory may still be in a preliminary stage in developing explanations of how advertising works. It is human to depend on what one knows, by either experience or analogy, and one develops ones thoughts in one or more less logical sequences from what channel what one knows and from the intellectual traditions that channel what one knows now towards what one would know in the future.

It is only in the recent years that the low-commitment formulation has developed, and it has yet to be either fully worked out or accepted.

In 1964, prior to the publication of Krugman's seminal paper, Jack B. Haskins bemoaned the state of the art: *"Why have communications been so resolute in presenting facts, and why have researchers been so persistent in measuring factual recall? One reason is that it is easy to do: it's easy to write a factual ad and it's easy to measure recall of facts. Another: the primary emphasis in our educational system has been to implant facts, through rote memorization, and so on, rather than to teach the students to think, reason, and relate. As the products of that system, we consciously or unconsciously build that approach into our efforts at mass communication."*

As of today, there are alternative explanations to the active learning theories of advertising that dominated practitioner and academic thought only a decade or two ago. The point is that not all the theoretical formulations, that are possible, may have been developed.

Only three of the six possible sequences involving learning, attitude change and behaviour have been seriously considered in the literature. Perhaps there are other elements of the advertising process beyond learning, attitude change and behaviour change, which could come into theoretical prominence in the years ahead. For example, the motivation to learn from advertising is assumed high in the active learning theories, irrelevant in the low-involvement theories and of moderate importance in the dissonance reduction theories. A new formulation, emphasising variation in motivational states as something important in consumer response to advertising, if were to come forward, could dramatically alter the shape of theory.

Demetrios Vakratsas and Tim Ambler (1999) reviewed more than 250 journal articles and books to establish what is and should be known about how advertising affects the consumer-how it works. They first deduced a taxonomy of models, discussed the theoretical principles of each class of models, and summarized their empirical findings. They then synthesized five generalizations about how advertising works and proposed directions for further research. Advertising effects were classified into intermediate effects, for example, on consumer beliefs and attitudes, and behavioural effects, which relate to purchasing behaviour, for example, on brand choice. The generalizations suggested that there was little support for any hierarchy, in the sense of temporal sequence, of effects. **The authors proposed that advertising effects should be studied in a space, with affect, cognition, and experience as the three dimensions.** Advertising's positioning in this space should be determined by context, which reflects advertising's goal diversity, product category, competition, other aspects of mix, stage of product life cycle, and target market.

Yuping (2019) repeated the effort, 20-years later, and focussed on online advertising has evolved significantly and now accounts for a substantial portion of all advertising spending. As online advertising tools proliferate, academic research in this area has also matured over time. To capture these developments, Yuping offered a synthesis of more than 300 articles on online advertising published in major advertising and marketing journals over the past 10 years. The key literature was summarized around six themes: (1) online advertising effectiveness; (2) online advertising mechanisms; (3) creative elements in online advertising; (4) the role of context in online advertising; (5) online personalization; and (6) search advertising. Knowledge gaps in existing research were identified, and important future research questions were suggested.

In the years ahead, significant advances in the current understanding of how advertising effects come about are expected. And, as experience has suggested, it would be not very wise to expect, that only those formulations of the advertising process that have developed so far would continue to be important in future.

The developing view about theory in advertising seems to be that no single theory will do for all cases of consumer- advertising interaction. In some situations, one theoretical approach may be appropriate, whereas in another situation, an alternative formulation may better fit reality. This developing view is we illustrated by the analysis of the alternative hierarchical formulations - learning response, low involvement and dissonance reduction-that were discussed here.

Michael L. Ray has made following observations about these three theories: *"Because each of three hypothesized orders of response is related to a particular research tradition, each is supported by theory and empirical evidence on the conditions under which it is elicited. A major thesis of this paper is that much will be gained by using the theory and results of all these approaches, rather than considering them as competitors."*

To the extent that this viewpoint is accepted, it will mark a significant departure in the development of advertising theory. In the past, individual theories have grown from a particular intellectual tradition and point of view, and their adherents have busily attempted to develop them into a single, all-encompassing explanation of the advertising process. It seems more probable that advertising effects are accomplished in a variety of ways and that it will be profitable, in the future, to investigate advertising as a multifaceted rather than as a single-faceted process.

This approach will open up a completely new area of theoretical and research concern, that is, how to define the boundaries between the various explanations of consumer or market response to advertising. Under precisely what conditions, for example, do active learning theories explain response to advertising? Under precisely what conditions and where, exactly, is the boundary line between advertising responses that are explained by the active learning theories and the low-involvement theories?

As theory develops, it should work its way back into practice. The way this is most likely to happen is through the process of evaluating finished advertisements.

New theoretical formulations will suggest new criteria upon which to judge the effectiveness of advertisements. As these are incorporated into research procedures and the implications of these research procedures and their theoretical base come to be understood in the community of advertising practitioners, change in practice will gradually unfold.

Until new theories become explicit in the research means of evaluating advertising, the new theories tend to remain theoretical formulations that have not demonstrated relevance to or connection with advertising practice.

Advertising: Production-Consumption Synchroniser

The control of time has become an essential requirement of the productive operations of the mass processes of a technological economy.
The mass process of advertising viewed in this technological context, perform a necessary balancing function by synchronising the process of mass consumption.

Advertising reduces the time between production and consumption by joining the technology of communications with the technology of manufacture. Advertising accelerates the demise of older, lower quality products by attracting consumers to modern, improved ones.

Effectiveness: A Function of Process Concept

In the above theoretical frameworks, the advertising process is viewed as having a cause-effect relationship. This is inadequate because discrepancies are bound to exist between what the advertiser presents in an ad (copy, message, sounds, visuals & execution) and what information and/or meaning the audience derive out of it. This can be attributed to the complexity of their needs, emotions, values and a host of other elements.

Bent Stidsen (1970) had formulated criteria to facilitate the appraisal of advertising effectiveness in terms of the marketing concept, taking into account the fulfilment of mutual objective of the consumer as the advertiser.

In doing so, he considers it necessary to study 'what people do to advertising' instead of 'what advertising does to people' because without their active involvement, advertising would be useless. Two-research system point of view and the other viewed from various approaches to the study of advertising process are detailed.

The consumers' communication system is defined as being made up of:
  a) What he knows (Awareness);
  b) What he reads, writes, listens, feels (input);
  c) Where he is going (goal-seeking);
  d) His standards for differentiating, accepting, rejecting data points and data spaces (integration); and
  e) The value and ideas he accept as being true, without question (Commitment).

PARADIGM FOR THE ADVERTISING PROCESS VIEWED FROM THE CONSUMER'S COMMUNICATION SYSTEM

		Physical Characteristics	Psycho-logical Characteristics	Functional Characteristics	Structural Characteristics	Moral Characteristics
Elements of Consumers' Communication System	Awareness	Conditions limiting or enabling communication.				
	Input System	Characteristics of channels or media used by the consumer for input purposes.				
	Goal Seeking	Purposes for which the consumer could, would, or feels, he should use advertising.				
	Integration	Standards used by the consumer for purposes of maintaining cognitive consistency.				
	Commitment	Values and ideas taken by the consumer to be unquestionably true.				

The advertising process could be thought of in terms of the followings:

a) Physical characteristics (techniques, media);

b) Psychological Characteristics (Perception, conception);

c) Functional characteristics (utility, purposes, economic values);

d) Structural characteristics (total campaign or a single ad.)

e) Moral or ethical characteristics (philosophy of advertising)

PARADIGM FOR THE ADVERTISING PROCESS VIEWED FROM APPROACHES TO THE STUDY OF ADVERTISING

		Physical Characteristics	Psychological Characteristics	Functional Characteristics	Structural Characteristics	Moral Characteristics
Elements of Consumers' Communication System	Awareness	Issues concerning distribution of messages to consumers	Issues concerning the process by which advertising and consumers create the meaning and importance of advertising	Issues concerning the costs and benefits of advertising	Issues concerning the institutional characteristics of advertising	Issues concerning the ethics or moral implications of advertising
	Input System					
	Goal Seeking					
	Integration					
	Commitment					

Super imposition of these two paradigms are expected to give a third, logically bounded one. The key features of this paradigm are:

a) *Each of the five different elements of an individual's communication system can be examined from five different and complementary angles.*

b) *The five approaches to the analysis and description of the advertising process would generate five different, yet complementary criteria for the assessment of advertising effectiveness.*

The implications of such an approach is, that the effectiveness would be a function of how one conceptualises the process. Secondly, advertising would be viewed as a phenomenon of human communication, meant for mutual benefits or buyers and sellers, efforts would be necessary to upgrade, modify in quality and quantity, and design advertising in a way that it becomes more and correctly informative. Its legitimacy needs to be protected and its effectiveness measured in the same manner as any management information system.

The above approach may not be revolutionary, yet it helps in changing some of the problems highlighted here though their elimination altogether is still far away.

3

Methods of Measuring Effectiveness of Advertising

Effectiveness is the extent to which an activity fulfils its intended purpose or function. Fraser (1994) defined it thus:

*"**Effectiveness**. This is a measure of the match between stated goals and their achievement. It is always possible to achieve 'easy', low-standard goals. In other words, quality in higher education cannot only be a question of achievements 'outputs' but must also involve judgements about the goals (part of 'inputs')"*

A quick glossary of inter-related terminology is here:

Effectiveness is a measure of the success in achieving a clearly stated objective.

Cost is the price, which has to be paid in achieving the objective. It can and should include subjective phenomena such as distress or discomfort.

Efficiency is cost effectiveness. The efficient solution is that which is most effective at least cost. Elements of marketing-mix (product, price, transaction & distribution systems) and promotional-mix (Advertising, publicity, personal selling and promotions directed towards consumers, channel partners and sales force) are the inputs deployed in order to achieve the desired objective.

Marketing Process is the sum of the activities to which inputs are subjected in order to achieve the objective. **Cost benefit** attempts to quantify the benefits and costs of different things. Neither inputs, processes nor outcomes are fixed; it is the resource available, which is predetermined and fixed. Cost benefit seeks, for example, to compare the costs and benefits of a price reduction rather than spending more on consumer promotions.

Outcomes - the measurement of effectiveness depends in the first instance upon the definition of outcome. The analogy with education is close; it is impossible to assess the results of teaching without setting educational objectives. Just as the setting of educational objectives influences a curriculum, the choice of outcome influences process.

Marketing strategy should lead to the setting of broad goals for advertising. The setting of these goals could include such things as, sales, preference, awareness, comprehension, attitudes or inquiries. Such goals must be distinguished from measurable and clear-cut objectives or outcomes.

Effectiveness, the evaluation of advertising, can be assessed only in relation to defined objectives; only the cumulative monitoring of effectiveness in achieving specific objectives can assess the achievement of goals.

Advertising Research

In the absence of a well-developed body of advertising theory, advertisers must make assumptions about the chain of events that take place between advertisement exposure and buying behaviour. Principal advertising decisions involve questions such as:

- a) To advertise or not to advertise;
- b) How much to spend on advertising;
- c) The message and its content;
- d) The media and their schedule.

Advertising Research means the systematic study of human beings either as senders or as receivers of overtly paid-for impersonal communication aiming at bringing about or facilitating purchase.

The field of Advertising Research may be subdivided as follows:

- a) Studies of the production of advertising (activities and routines within or between advertising institutions such as producers, advertising agencies and media)
- b) normative studies of marketing management
- c) empirical studies of advertising as a business function (effects of advertising on product awareness, attitudes, intentions to buy, and purchases)
- d) Studies of social effects of advertising (effects not directly intended).

Arndt (1976) has given a scheme for the various kinds of Advertising Research activity that is usually undertaken.

EFFECT MEASURES	NATURE OF THE STIMULI Stimulus functioning on a		
	short-term basis		long-term basis
	One Stimulus	Several Stimulus	Stimulus Clusters may be applicable
1. No Effect Measures	Check Costs	Content Analysis	Historical Content Analysis
2. One Phase in a Decision Process	a) Motivation Research b) Audience Measurement Studies c) Laboratory Studies d) Simple Survey Studies e) Aggregate Studies of Advertising-Sales Relationship	-	a) Longitudinal Laboratory Studies b) Panel Studies
3. Several Thesis in a Decision Process	Cumulative Effect Studies	Diffusion of Innovation Studies	Diffusion of Innovation Studies
4. Several Decision Process	-	Usage and Gratification Studies	a) Consumer Socialisation Studies b) Life Style Studies

The Premises of Advertising Research

The vast majority of advertising research is purposeful and useful in practitioner terms but it is not clearly related to the ultimate effects of the advertising that is tested. Because of this ambiguity, it is important to summarize the premises that underlie contemporary advertising research for developing advertisement and advertising campaigns.

1   There is an unknown. The practitioner wants to know something and believes that a research measurement will be better than his own guess or intuition.

2   The correct unknown has been identified. The practitioner believes that what he wants to know will be more helpful to him than other things he might want to know. Practitioners do not always agree about how advertising works and thus do not always agree about what they need to know to make better advertising, or appraise what they have done.

Alfred Politz (1961) clarifies this premise that individual advertisers identify key unknowns that are meaningful to them:

> "... if someone thinks that the ability of advertising to attract attention is directly related to its effectiveness, he will then, of course, measure the attention getting ability and consider the results to be a measure of advertising effectiveness. If someone thinks the fact that an advertising phrase is remembered signifies effectiveness, he will use memory measurements as a criterion of performance. If someone believes that advertising has to give pleasure and be liked, he may then subject the pleasantness or the aesthetic values to measurement and will interpret a positive result as proof of the effectiveness of the advertising. In each case the researcher calls upon an implicit assumption about the mechanisms by which advertising achieves its effect."

The important point is that the practitioner believes, when he undertakes research, that whatever unknown he specifies is more meaningful to him, as a practitioner, than are other unknowns that he may specify.

3   **The process of advertising research will yield data that make the specified unknown, known.** This premise implies that advertising research can be depended upon in specific ways:

   a) *Advertising research data collection procedures are valid.* That is, the data yielded by the research procedure do, in fact, describe the relation of consumers to the specified unknown.

   b) *Research data collection procedures are reliable.* That is, the procedure will give the same answer when a measurement is repeated under reasonably comparable circumstances.

   c) *Advertising research data collection procedures are sensitive.* That is, if a small but real difference exists between consumer attitudes about a brand, or consumer reactions to an advertisement, the research procedure will reflect that small difference, but will not report that it is a large difference or that no different exists.

   d) *Consumer research sampling procedures yield valid estimates of population values.* That is, sampling procedures are valid and can be depended upon, day in and day out, to produce actionable data.

4   **Relative measurements are valuable.** If an absolute measurement, such as the percentage of people exposed to an advertisement who can recall it, is of little relevance, relative measurements are acceptable. Thus, if we know that 30% of all people exposed to a television commercial for an automobile can recall the

commercial, we do not know very much. But if we know that the average memory recall for all automobile commercials is 15% and that the highest recall score ever attained by an automobile commercial is 32%, our knowledge is vastly increased.

5   *It is worth delaying decisions in order to have research results.* Thus, the practitioner is willing to trade the time required to do the research, for the research results.

6   *Repeated standard measurements are valuable*. Even though advertisements differ, and product promises differ, and advertising media differ, they are sufficiently similar among themselves to justify repeated standard measurements of the same kind. Practitioners know that standard concept tests, or standard attitude measures, or standard media audience measures may short change or over value some advertisements, or some concepts or some media, but they are willing to accept this shortcoming of standardized procedure for comparability and continuity in measurement. Special or one-of-a-kind measurements tend to be hard to interpret, because the results are absolute.

7   *The effects of advertisements, advertising concepts, and advertising media change over time*, and thus advertising research-based knowledge wears out. Advertising research tends to involve the continuous measurement of discrete advertising events. As Charles Ramond (1976) says:

> *"There are virtually no permanent data in advertising research-only data that stay true long enough to permit a decision to be taken in the knowledge that its consequences will be realized before the facts on which it rests have changed. For practical budgeting purposes, this time interval is usually set at one year."*

The practitioner who authorises and uses advertising research accepts these premises, even if he is unable to state them explicitly. He is indifferent to the intricacies of research procedure as such and, in the main, depends upon the advertising researcher to tend to the research issues and to deliver an acceptable research product within the boundaries set by the premises. For example, the advertising practitioner accepts the principles of sampling that underlie survey research procedure and holds the advertising researcher responsible for developing and executing an adequate sample plan. Alternatively, the advertising practitioner accepts responsibility for identifying the proper unknown and expects the advertising researcher to find an adequate measurement of that unknown.

In the final analysis practitioners use advertising research because they hope and expect that it will improve the quality of their advertising and improve it at least to an extent that will recoup the costs of the research itself. But it is often hard to prove that research does, in fact, lead to such improvements. As Mark Albion and Paul Farris (1979) write:

> *"It is reasonable to suppose that companies investing time and money in activities designed to aid the development of advertising messages and/or test the consumer responses of advertisements before they actually purchase space or time are likely to have more effectiveness is significant enough to result in appreciable economies is an open question."*

Some Typical Advertising Effects

Advertising has multiple effects. Some intended, others are not. This stems primarily from the fact that there are multiple objectives of advertising, the exposure is to audience some of which is not included in the target and that advertising seems to work in more ways than it is anticipated to work or intended to work.

Consumer Effects of Advertising

Advertising obviously can and does have many effects on consumers, including

a) Verbal responses on
   (i) The ways in which people answer questions about the ad, saying whether they:
   - Recall seeing or hearing the ad.
   - Liked or were influenced by the ad.

   (ii) The way in which people answer questions about the product, saying whether they :
   - are familiar with the product.
   - express favourable opinions about the product
   - express an intention to buy the product
   - have bought the product.

b) Non-verbal Responses on
   (i) The ways in which people actually behave (nonverbal) toward the product:
   - the choices they make in a laboratory situation;
   - Whether or not they shopped for the product and inquired about it;
   - Whether or not they purchased the product;
   - how much of the product they purchased;
   - the ways in which they used the product.

   (ii) The physiological and physical response of the people.

The above list is not intended to be complete. It is meant only to indicate the range of ways in which advertising might affect consumers.

Trade Effects of Advertising

A consumer advertising campaign, by its impact on members of the trade, could effect:

- a) The readiness with which the company's representative are received and the ease of their selling job;
- b) The purchase of the product by the trade;
- c) The frequency and magnitude with which the trade promotes the product;
- d) The attitudes of people in the trade;
- e) The price that the trade is willing to pay for the product.

This is a partial list only of the possible trade effects of consumer advertising.

Other Effects of Advertising:

- a) The use of an advertising campaign may effect the nature of competitive actions. For example, budget increases may be matched or exceeded by competitors. A particularly strong theme, or the use of an unusual medium, may cause a direct response by the competition.
- b) Employees of the company may be affected by its advertising. A campaign emphasising product quality may cause production workers to be more careful about quality. Similarly, a campaign stressing new uses for product may motivate salesperson to focus their presentations toward new ways to use the product.
- c) In addition, other people in society, government, financial Institutions, and so on, may be affected either positively or negatively by an advertising campaign. As a result, their anticipated and actual reactions any affect various aspects of the company's activities.

Measuring Effectiveness of Advertising

In order to use any measure of effectiveness of advertising, it is necessary to take into account the degree and direction of change that may take place in the market due to variations in the pattern of demand and supply and in buyer behaviour as well as a result of the promotional efforts of the advertisers. One should take into account all possible direct and indirect substitutes for the product or service in question.

In the first place there has to be clarity in deciding what one must aim at measuring and also specifying the types of measurement required. Any evaluation of an advertising campaign will depend on the objectives of the campaign. Basic question regarding the overall objectives of promotional strategy and of a particular campaign under review should be asked:

a) What influenced the setting of these objectives?

b) How can the achievements of these objectives be measured?

A description of the various methods which can be used for measuring the effectiveness of an advertising campaign will be dysfunctional without a reference to the circumstances in which a technique becomes applicable.

Advertising Objectives and Plans

The setting of advertising objectives should be followed by defining and prioritising the expectations of the advertiser from an advertising programme. This should be feasible considering that advertising objectives are expected to be in line with the firm's marketing objectives, which in turn are derived from the overall corporate objectives.

Advertising programmes vary widely with regard to the mix of promotional ingredients. Some firms, for instance, may omit personal selling and use direct mail advertising as a sole promotional tool, and omitting mass media advertising completely. The result that advertisers generally want from their effort is an increase in the marketing performance parameters such as sales, market shares and profits. Immediate sale may be expected from direct mailing and retail store advertising.

The role of advertising however, will be quite different in the marketing of items like heavy machinery, where it may help build an image for the company as a reliable supplier of machinery, to encourage enquiries and to make it easier for the salespersons of the company to get a good reception.

Lack of clarity in setting advertising objectives may arise due to the following factors (Corkindale and Kennedy 1976):

a) Problem in stating objectives in quantifiable terms
b) Apparent failures in realising that results of advertising cannot generally be measured in terms of sales.
c) Inadequate information about media, its qualitative focus and its reach.

The actual forms which advertising objectives can take area extremely diverse. Various communication goals, in varying situations might be related to a single advertisement, an entire campaign for a product or a company's overall advertising philosophy.

Another way of looking at advertising objectives is in relation to the hierarchy of psychological processes. Considering all advertising motivation as psychological in nature, the testing methods would also rely on psychological measurement techniques. Some of the important categories of psychological elements of advertising objectives cited include initial attention, reception, continuance of favourable attitudes or interest, recall and recognition, comprehension, feelings, emotions, motivations, beliefs, intentions, imagery, association and other basic or situational decision parameters (Lucas and Britt 1950).

The overall purpose of advertising in any situation must be defined first and then broken down into various stages. The development of advertising goals, and a sound basis for evolving an evaluation framework, can be aided by thinking of the following five stages in a purchase decision (Wolfe, Brown and Thompson 1962).

Areas of Assessment of Effectiveness

A meaningful measurement of the effectiveness of advertising will be possible only by disaggregating the total area to be covered and relating it to various stages of processing and proportion of advertising and the hierarchy of its possible effects. Research techniques may accordingly be applied at four stages.

> a) A continuous analysis of past advertising experience in search of guidelines for an analytical framework is a very useful first step except in the case of new advertisers or new products. Such an analysis can provide a valuable basis for reviewing and developing advertising strategy.
>
> b) Surveys of buyer behaviour and consumer preference are helpful in developing advertising objectives and strategy. Such research will also be useful in monitoring changes in the target market segment.
>
> c) The third area involves pretesting advertisements before their release. This is a very important part in the evaluation

of advertising effectiveness. Pre-testing provides an indication of the likely acceptance of an advertisement or a campaign by the target audience.

Results of pre-testing will obviously be used for making improvements and changes as suggested by research. It will also bring forth limitations, if any. Since the media costs account for most of the cost of advertising, a qualitative as well as quantitative evaluation of media may also be required.

d) The post-test research involves testing of reach and impact of advertising after it has been released. Pre-production research and post-testing are complementary. The former is diagnostic and is concerned with what should be said or shown, the latter is concerned with evaluation of notability, recognition, recall, comprehension and behavioural changes, if any, brought about by the advertising.

An ideal measure of advertising effectiveness would be on measurement of these seven attributes:

a) Scope of advertising being measured
b) expected audiences response
c) realistic conditions of test exposure
d) precision and tolerance of measurement
e) representativeness of sample measured
f) methods of comparison against what standard
g) data handling procedures.

This would be called IMP-Idealised Measurement Procedure (Dalbey, Gross and Wind 1968).

Pre-Placement Evaluation of Advertising

Although past experience and a 'feel' for the market would always remain valuable aids for advertising executives, a systematic and methodical approach for estimating the possible effectiveness of the advertising before its release would be a worthwhile effort and might also be helpful in avoiding possible adverse effects later.

One of the first advertising decisions may require searching and screening of suitable advertising ideas. This may entail:

a) the quest for new ideas or for new expressions of old ones

b) the collection of facts about what people know or feel about a company

c) the prediction of how people will probably react to a new advertising idea.

Testing of creative approaches and themes prior to development of creative strategy can give the earliest indication of effectiveness. Themes, product ideas, brand names, slogans and other elements to be included in an advertisement can be thus evaluated.

Concept Testing

A major feature of creative strategy that has a bearing on ultimate effectiveness of advertising is the basic communication concept around which a campaign may be developed. For instance, Lipton Green Label is a premium variety tea and is the brand leader in the Darjeeling packed tea market. The campaign introduced in 1981 emphasised the environmental features of the area, such as the shade of Himalayas and cool mountain winds where this tea is grown.

Concept testing would usually involve not more than 50 to 100 respondents, using techniques such as qualitative interviews, free association tests and various statement comparison tests.

Qualitative interviews of an informal nature may be conducted individually or in groups from amongst people drawn from a cross-section of ages, sexes, occupations and income levels that may represent the audience for the advertisement in question.

Free-association tests are used to pick up secondary associations to names or key words. These tests are conducted by having respondents mention the first thing they think of when a given name is mentioned.

Colgate Palmolive in India decided to introduce a detergent cake under the brand name Fab. At the stages of initial test marketing of this product, one could conceive a free association test for the name Fab, considering that an orange flavour soft drink under the name was already in the market. The test could give an indication of the spontaneous association of a name like Fab with washing material in India, although Fab is a brand name used by the parent company for detergent powder.

Statement comparison tests are used when testing various concepts on small groups. *The Rank-order method* required respondents to rank the different concepts or themes indicating their preference or desirability in relation to the product.

The paired comparison method requires the respondents to determine which of the two concepts is preferred, using a series of pairs of statements association with product related concepts and characteristics.

The Absolute Comparison method involves the comparison of each of the concepts against an absolute standard. For example, an advertiser has the option of highlighting certain features of the products and services advertised. Ratings may be obtained from a sample of the audience on an interval scale regarding those features. These ratings may then be used for selecting features of high interest value as compared with the minimum essential features that could serve as the benchmark for comparison.

Theme and Slogan Testing

No specific guidelines are available for classifying themes for the purpose of analysis and research. Mohan (1982) has attempted a classification of advertising themes under the following categories:

Utilitarian	:	emphasis on the value of the product and/or service; directed towards providing satisfaction for the money or effort spent on obtaining the product/service.
Focused	:	an extension of utilitarian themes; which will appeal to specific market/audience segments.
Informative	:	emphasis only on the information about the product/service being advertised while no explicit selling message is present.
Non-Specific	:	A vague or diffused message that contains only passing references to products or advertisers.
Achievement Orientation	:	highlighting the achievements in terms of sales, profits or awards won by the advertiser.
Descriptive & Projective	:	a combination of Informative and Achievement Oriented themes.
New Product, service, or idea	:	A new entry in the Market
Contributory to economy or industry	:	mainly relevant to institutional advertising, emphasising the contributions made by the advertiser towards industrial growth and economic development.

It may be noted that a theme and a slogan are not the same.

A slogan always says the same thing in exactly the same way, for example, *"Hamara Bajaj"* (Bajaj Scooters) and *"Taste the Thunder"* (Thums Up). The unchanging nature of a slogan offers advantages in its own right and its constant repetition in unaltered form usually enables it to become so closely associated with a company name that the slogan can almost substitute the brand name.

Motivation research techniques such as depth interviews and group discussions, apart from structured tests may be used for pre-testing of themes.

The Media Factor

The best of messages may fail in achieving their objectives, if the message vehicle is inappropriate or inadequate in terms of its reach and coverage. In addition to having a major bearing on the cost of advertising, media types and advertising vehicles can influence advertising effectiveness in three ways (Wolfe et.al. 1966).

    a) They determine in large measure the size and characteristics of the audience exposed to advertising; that is, how many and what types of persons would have an opportunity to see or hear the advertising, and how often they would see or hear it.

    b) They provide an environment that is favourable, unfavourable or neutral for advertising copy and the products features and/or affect the probability that the advertisement will be seen or heard.

    c) In interaction with copy and the audience, they determine the overall impact of an advertising campaign-the information communicated, the attitudes formed or changed, or the action that may be taken as a result of advertising.

These media related influences taken alone, and in combination with cost data, are frequent subjects of media research.

Media Research

An advertiser may take the following steps before undertaking media research and using media research data gathered by others, as media selection and scheduling are obviously linked with the accomplishment of advertising objectives, linked with the accomplishment of advertising objectives, which in turn are intended to support the marketing objectives.

a) Media objectives should be set. The character of media, the size of the profile the audience, the overall environment, the expected contribution of the media or the specific media vehicle to the total impact of a campaign, would determine these objectives.

b) The target audience for the advertiser's specific product and brand or a particular campaign should be defined in advance;

c) The management may indicate the relative advertising weight or proportion of the advertising budget to be allocated to each campaign or programme.

d) Any constraints such as frequency of appearance of media, its availability and its reach should be fully taken into account.

Wolfe and co-authors refer to seven key areas of media research.

a) Ability of media to reach households who are in the market for an advertiser's products/services/ideas.

b) Opportunity for exposure to the advertising on any media under consideration by those members of a household who influence the purchase decisions.

c) Extent of the conscious impression the advertising message in a specific media makes on an individual.

d) Ability of the advertising message placed in a specific media to change favourably the attitude of the individual toward product/services or idea promoted.

e) Ability of the attitude charge caused by the advertising message in a specific media to create purchasing intention or to modify it.

f) Extent of the action that the advertising message in the specific medium evokes on the part of the individual through prompting a visit to the purchase point, or being receptive to a sales call.

g) Determination of the additional sales of the advertised product that a message in a specific media provided.

Copy Research

The basic purpose of pretesting of various possible advertisements is to establish whether the message content and its presentation are likely to perform their allocated task efficiently, and what changes or improvements may be helpful.

Pre-tests should be conducted in the following situations:

a) To substitute on ongoing campaign with a new campaign

b) To introduce a product, or a brand

c) When there are uncertainties or contradictory views expressed about the content of an advertisement.

A pre-test may be carried out employing relatively small samples. It is, however, important to simulate the actual environment as the one in which the audience would read, see or hear the advertisement. This is especially relevant to the protesting of television advertising.

A PROGRAM OF METHODS DEVELOPMENT RESEARCH

Area	Advertiser's Decision	What is Measured	Methods under Study	Methodological Goal	Advertising Goal
Motivation Research	What to say	Consumer Motives	Non-directed interviews, projective techniques	Cheaper way of measuring buying motives	New appeals
Copy Research	How to say it	Recall, recognition of ads.	Mail questionnaires (post-tests) Theatre Tests (pre-tests)	Adequate pre- and post- tests of ad. memorability	More memorable ads.
Visual Research	How to show it	Response to visual displays	Tachistoscopic devices	Company-wide visual rating service	Higher impact for all forms of visual communication
Media Research	Where to say it	Audience size and composition	Re-analyses of existing surveys	Accurate two-year forecasts	Best buys within and between media
Public Opinion Research	To whom to say it	Attitudes, demographic characteristics	Personal interviews	Identification of definable attitude groups	Correct audience for institutional advertising
Operations Research	How much to spend	Relationship between advertising expenditure and sales	Mathematical models	Successful prediction of sales in test markets	Optimal size and allocation of ad budgets

Courtesy: Advertising Research Section, E. I. Du Pont de Nemours & Co., Inc.

Various methods and devices of pretesting, currently in use, are listed in above. Various parameters on which measurements are possible and the corresponding methods of protesting are indicated. Since advertisements may generate both physiological and psychological responses, measurement techniques cover both. Some of the common methods are directed below:

Consumer Jury

The technique involves an assembly of several people who represent views of potential consumers. These individuals are shown the advertisements or commercials and their comments on specific elements of content and creative approach are obtained. A variation to this procedure is made by having a panel of individuals who can be interviewed at their respective places in order to obtain individual opinions which can later be collected to obtain a representative conclusion.

Matched Samples

Two or more groups of persons comparable in respect of parameters such as age, sex, income occupation, behavioural characteristics and product usage as relevant to the research problem constitute matched samples.

The testing procedure involves showing one variation of the pre-test advertising or copy, to one group and another variation to a matched group. The variations may be made in any of the elements viz. themes, headlines, slogans, visuals and body copy.

"Before" and "after" measures of perceptions regarding specific issues are administered and any major changes between the control and the matched groups may be attributed to the differences in the version being tested since all other conditions may be assumed to be similar.

Portfolio Tests

The method consists is collecting several advertisements in a portfolio with typical editorial contents. Each of these advertisements is for a different product.

The portfolio is then individually shown to a representative sample of respondents who are expected to flip through it just the way they would have looked through a magazine or a newspaper. The respondent is then asked to recall the advertisements and any other relevant details.

This gives an indication of the extent of recall of the product and the advertisements under extent of recall of the product and the advertisements under test, as well as of elements of content. Additional measurements of attitudinal parameters may also be made. The portfolio test may be used with matched samples of respondents in order to study the variations in the advertisements contained in a similar portfolio.

Story-board tests

A procedure similar to the portfolio testing can be used for film or television advertisements. It involves developing story-boards into film strips or video cassettes. Filmstrip story-boards may be shown as single frames. Respondents are usually shown 8 to 10 such experimental advertisements.

Following the screening, measurement of recall of products and brands and retention and comprehension of messages may be made. Respondents may also be asked to make observations on the qualitative features.

Mechanical and other devices

There are two types of mechanical devices; those controlling the exposure and others providing praise measurement of responses. Some of the more common devices are the following.

Tachistoscope is a timing device as the one used in cameras. It allows the operator to regulate the viewing time of an advertisement or a package design. Tests of recognition are administered to representative samples of target audience. They may also be asked to comment on the distinctive features of the test advertisement or package and items of immediate visual significance such as design and colour scheme. A portable version of Tachistoscope can be made for carrying test at homes of respondents.

Eye-movement Cameras are devices that record the amount of time subjects spend looking at advertisement and the path of eye travel from one element of an advertisement to another.

Pupilometric devices record the changing dilation of a subject's pupil while viewing a print advertisement or an advertising film. These changes give an indication of attention value of an advertisement and related emotional responses (Krugman 1964).

Psycho-galvanic response measures are made through devices that record change in electrical conductivity. Emotional excitement causes increased sweat secretions that lead to an increase in electrical conductivity of skin and these increases are recorded by psycho-galvanometer. A lie detector is based on the same basic principle and psychogalvanic response can provide an accurate measure of the attention catching value of a test advertisement.

Use of pre-test results

All pretesting techniques described above have certain limitations. There is no established theory of how advertising works. Pretesting can offer only a limited, nevertheless, valuable indication of what test advertisements including promotional features such as package designs, can achieve. Differences in the pretest setting and the actual situation of exposure to advertising can make a substantial impact on overall effectiveness of advertising and should be taken into account while selecting and designing the tests and interpreting results.

Post-testing

Post-testing aims at ascertaining the extent to which advertising achieves its specified objectives following its release. This aspect of evaluation of effectiveness of an advertisement or a campaign, can serve as a valuable feedback provided testing is undertaken by keeping the objectives of advertising in view. The common practice of treating incremental sales during the period of advertising as being the outcome of advertising is not valid in most cases. The factors effecting sales are so numerous that they defy measurement. In many cases, it may be more relevant and meaningful to limit post-testing to various stages in the buying process such as creation of the awareness of a brand, development of favourable attitudes towards a brand or changes in knowledge about an organization or disposition towards it.

Measure of Audience Exposures

The mere fact that consumers subscribe to certain publications or listen to certain programmes does not mean that they notice or remember the advertisements they contain. There are organizations in the United States that provide information on the exposure of readers of magazines to advertising. Two such well-known syndicated services are Daniel Starch and Gallup Robinson. These organisations are tying up with Indian Market Research Organisations to conduct similar syndicated studies in India.

Daniel Starch (1966), a pioneer in advertising research, started collection of audience exposure data for selected American publications since 1930's. Of course, these publications have varied over years due to changes in their popularity and circulation. Known as *Starch ratings*, the data is provided under three headings *"Noted"*, *"Seen-Associated"* and *"Read-Most"*. Interviewers visit respondents at their houses and ask if they have read certain magazines. Readers of the concerned magazines are then asked to review page by page the advertisement they remember having seen.

"Noted" score refers to the percentage of respondents who indicate having looked at an advertisement. *"Seen-Associated"* score refers to those who had looked at the brand name or realised that the advertisement was for a particular product. The *"Read-Most"* score refers to those who indicated that they had read most of the advertisement. Cost data on the number of readers per dollar and the cost per reader reached compared with the competition are also provided in the Starch reports.

The other research organisation, Gallup-Robinson provide a service for measuring the impact of an advertisement based on recall. Consumers who have read certain magazines are identified and asked to recall the brand names from the advertisements they have see. The score based on this data has been termed as the Proved Name Registrations, PNR. Information about specific copy points is also sought from them. That may help in determining those copy points that seem to have made the greatest impression. This information is valuable for the advertiser and the agency in developing subsequent advertisements and campaigns (Faison 1980).

Measuring Attitudes and Attitude Change

Advertising is aimed at creating favourable impression for company and its products and the results may be measured by attitudinal studies. The relationship of attitudes to product usage may be a more significant measure of advertising effectiveness as against awareness and recall studies.

Psychological Measurement techniques may be used to explore feelings below the conscious level. Probes into the unconscious reveal the mental "environment" in which the advertising must do its work. This could perhaps, give clues to the types of advertising approaches that would prove most acceptable in achieving specified objectives. Various techniques that can be used in such attitudinal studies include Depth Interviews, focused Group Interviews, Derivations of Thematic Apperception Tests and Projective Tests Lovell and Potter 1975).

Analysing Sales and Product Usage

The correlation of sales to advertising can be meaningful measure of effectiveness in providing simultaneous impact of factors like product quality, selling effort, brand prestige, distribution channels, their reach and loyalty, buyer attitudes or inertia, competitive situation, size and location of displays, discount policies, delivery, seller services can be isolated. The sales effects of advertising can be most accurately estimated under the following conditions (Ramond 1970).

> a) The product or brand has no direct substitute, now or in the future. Competing products are few and technology is

unlikely to make the item obsolete during the period of experimentation.

b) The buyers of the product can be unambiguously defined, can be reached easily by advertising and interviewers and are geographically concentrated.

c) The lot size of the purchase remains unchanged from purchase to purchase by the same buyer, and between one buyer and another.

d) The period is constant over time, market and quantity purchased.

e) Channels of distribution are adequate. The more channels there are, the less unlikely the consumer is to be frustrated in an advertising induced attempt to buy.

f) Levels of distribution are adequate. The more wholesalers, dealers and distribution stand between the producer and consumer, more the individuals must decide before purchase can occur and the more levels there are that need to be influenced by advertising.

g) The influence of personal selling is constant over time and over markets.

h) Competitors' technical services do not differ substantially from those of the advertisers.

i) The copy platform is constant and clear. The fewer the copy planks, the easier it is to tell whether communication has occurred.

j) Special promotions are not undertaken.

k) Packaging is distinctive and remains unaltered.

Methods of Measuring Effectiveness Of Advertising

l) The Producer is the only advertiser of the brand -- that is, there is no cooperative or local advertising.

m) Competitors are slow to respond to changes in the advertiser's marketing strategy and maintain the same marketing policies.

n) Competitors' advertising and marketing policies are relatively constant in all markets.

o) Potential sales can be accurately estimated for small geographical units and during short time periods such as weeks or months.

p) Government controls over product design, price, competition and advertising are minimal or at least not subject to rapid changes.

Depending on the fulfilment of the above conditions, measures of changes in an outlet's share of company's business and changes in a brand's share of the market may be made. It must also be noted that the appropriate measures of sales will relate to sales made to the final buyer and not by the company to its first point of sale. In the case of most consumer products, such data may be obtained from retail audit surveys that are conducted on a continuing basis. The Operations Research Group (ORG) in India used to collects and provides such data. Today, there are numerous firms in this service.

Enquiries and Returns

Advertising may be aimed at generating orders, inquiries, requests for information or getting a request for a salesperson to make in a call. By classifying replies to links included in advertisements, seeming effectiveness of advertising in different media may be evaluated.

Controlled Field Experiments

Controlled field experiments simulate the approach of laboratory experiments and are run under realistic conditions.

Split-run is a known technique used for print advertising. Research consists in using two versions of an advertisement that are prepared and inserted in the same issue of a magazine or a newspaper. However, the two versions are carried by two different sets of copies, some of which are meant for delivery in one location/area and the remaining in a `matched' location in terms of relevant audience characteristics. This experiment can be used to measure the immediate effectiveness of advertising by comparing the difference in sales between the two areas for the product advertised. The technique is obviously more relevant for consumer products that have a high recency of purchase and sales data may be analysed for short periods, say on a weekly.

Other Methods

Sometimes other methods are also used for measuring the results of advertising.

    a) *Playback audit*: is a means of verifying the wholesalers and retails salespersons' use of advertising themes or phrases in their own selling efforts. In this method, interviewers pose as prospective purchasers of the advertised product to see what advertising themes are played back by the salesperson in their sales presentation.

    b) *Analysis of secondary effects*: This involves measuring some related secondary effect and not the sales. For example, in case of advertising that not only promotes a product but offers free maintenance service; variations in requests for maintenance service may prove to be a good indicator of the impact of advertising and a more appropriate measure than sales.

c) *Analysis of reader's use of advertising*: may be used by retail stores and other agencies that distribute promotional literature/material such as catalogues. They try to find out the actual use to which the advertising is put to by the people, assuming that such action indicates the interest of the audience.

Limitations in Post-testing

A partial measurement of advertising results is usually possible. However, measuring all effects of advertising may not be feasible. Some of the results of advertising such as development of brand preferences and loyalties and repeat purchase of a brand in the case of products having low usage rate take time to show up and may not be traceable to specific advertisements. These results need to be measured over long periods of time, during which the changes occurring in other marketing parameters might invalidate the results.

There is obviously, considerable need to expand the application of various methods of measurement and equally numerous are the problems and unresolved issues in such effort. Some of the major problems of research in the effectiveness of advertising are:

a) *Frequency effects*: Does scheduling spacing and timing of advertisements contribute to their effectiveness?

b) Is there a *threshold of advertising expenditure* that, if not reached, will render such advertising largely ineffective?

c) What is the *rate at which advertisements wear out*? How many different advertisements should be made for a campaign? For how long is campaign useful?

d) The unresolved dilemma over the effectiveness of the 'continuous' or the 'intermittent' flow of advertising. Should a 'big' impact or a continuous presence be made periodically? The execution of advertising is a very important factor in its overall effectiveness. Krugman suggests that multiple exposures over a short period of time may lead to confusion in the minds of target audience that may result in a diffused message (Krugman 1977).

e) Will a change in attitudes prompt a change in behaviour? Are attitudinal changes necessary and possible through advertising?

Interpretation of Research Findings

A lot of research has gone into improving the accuracy of the measurement of the effectiveness of advertising and much can be done by following an objective and methodical approach. The whole purpose of the effort is not just an improvement in the measurement of effectiveness but obviously in mailing the advertising itself more effective.

Some points for consideration in this context are the following:

a) It is a big assumption that a favourable consumer attitude will lead to desired buying behaviour, which may not be wholly true (Mitchel and Olson 1981).

b) Sales objectives are basically marketing objectives and they cannot be realised by advertising alone. Relating sales to advertising without a reference to other factors may be unrealistic (Brown 1974).

Application of Effectiveness Research

The measurement of effectiveness of advertising must be cost-effective. The need for evaluating has to be appraised in terms of information gained. Although the value of intuition and judgment cannot be denied, objectivity in measurement cannot also be relegated to a less important place. A small advertiser is more prone to using a subjective approach, often because of resource constraints and the level of comprehension of the need for such research and the capability of interpreting it and using it in a fruitful manner. An advertiser must go in for a unique advertising strategy according to the individual situation of a product. Copying or reacting to a competitor's activities without a reference to one's own marketing and advertising objectives may be suicidal (Vaughm 1981).

Improving on Effectiveness of Advertising

It is important to note that the study of effectiveness of advertising is a joint responsibility of an advertiser and its advertising agency, regardless of who is paying for research and under what head of account it is allocated. A proper understanding of various aspects of effectiveness requires continuity of observation and use of appropriate research, as and when called for. There can be a strong temptation to pass superficial judgment on the so-called effectiveness of an advertisement or a campaign. It is, however, quite possible that a campaign may have proved effective owing to intrinsic merit and appropriateness or favourable conditions or a combination of both.

Advertising effectiveness should not be confused with the winning of awards such as those given by the Advertising Club, Bombay in coordination with the Commercial Artists' Guild. These All India awards for excellence in advertising have the following guidelines for judging the entries:

- a) Attention value
- b) Comprehensibility
- c) Credibility
- d) Technical execution
- e) Overall impact
- f) Originality

The jury for such awards evaluate the entries on the basis of their knowledge and experience and obviously no research can be used. An award winning entry may however, have the makings of an effective advertisement.

Improvements in effectiveness of advertising can be brought about by careful and considered changes introduced through combined efforts of an advertiser and the advertising agency because both marketing and advertising considerations have to be taken into account while evaluating the effectiveness of advertising. Requisite research provides the basis for the specific situations as well as for an objective comparison with earlier experiences and can help considerably in making better decisions regarding various aspects of advertising.

———

4

A Fresh Take on Advertising Effects

Advertising Research is far from an exact science. This is because of lack of reliability in the research procedures. This problem has been well established in the earlier discussions. With the existing research techniques, it is possible to do a reasonable job of determining *"what the advertising communicates?"* but that does not give one any idea what so ever as regards *"what to communicate?"* and *"why communicate that?"*; so as to maximise the odds that the advertising becomes effective. This may better be determined before the advertising is created and not after it is released.

That advertising is communication is well accepted, but why advertise and why communicate, what is expected to be achieved due to advertising or communication. What makes one sure that advertising or communication would achieve the purpose they are intended to.

The discussions in the preceding chapter focused on the current line of thought in so far as advertising works in shaping attitudes of audience towards the advertised product or theme. Attitudes are supposed to be made up of two components, the salient attributes expected in the object and some kind of importance ascribed to these attributes.

Fishbein's Attitude Model

Fishbein's now-familiar attitude model (1963, 1967) specifies the relationship between the set of salient beliefs about a concept (often termed cognitive structure) and an overall evaluation of, or attitude toward, the concept.

$$\sum_{i=1}^{n} b_i \, e_i = A_o$$

Where:

b_i = the strength of the association between the attitude concept, and the ith salient concept.

e_i = the evaluation of, or attitude toward concept o,

and

n = the number of salient beliefs.

Fishbein clearly intended the attitude model in this equation to describe only the predicted relationship between measures of the theoretical constructs (Fishbein and Ajzen 1975). That is, the algebraic model provides a means of estimating the belief-attitude relationship that was formed because of causal mechanisms. The model itself does not "state" the causal proposition nor does it specify the causal mechanisms.

Fishbein also proposed that the attitude-belief relationship specified in the above equation holds for attitudes toward a specific behaviour such as buying a product, A_{act}. However, the set of salient beliefs may not be the same as for A_o. In turn, attitude, especially A_{act}, is presumed to have a causal influence on behavioural intentions (BI). In sum, Fishbein proposed a causal flow among three cognitive variables -

beliefs, evaluations or attitudes, and intentions (Lutz 1977). According to this view, marketing stimulus such as an advertisement affects consumers' beliefs first. Then the influenced salient beliefs mediate the marketing variable's effect on attitude, and attitude in turn mediates subsequent effects on behavioural intention.

The basic theoretical proposition of Fishbein's attitude theory is that beliefs cause attitude. Because attitude is determined by a set of salient beliefs, changes in attitude must be mediated by changes in those beliefs. Therefore, to change a person's attitude toward a concept, one must modify the salient beliefs about that concept.

Beliefs can be modified by changing the strength of a salient belief (b_i), changing the evaluation of a belief (e_i), creating a new salient belief, or making a salient belief non-salient (Lutz 1975). Fishbein's algebraic model then can be used to estimate the subsequent effect on overall attitude. Our key concern is with the proposition that beliefs cause attitudes. Stated in its strongest sense, the presumption is that beliefs mediate all effects on attitude formation or attitude change.

Developing an empirical test of this causal relationship is straightforward, at least logically. Assume that a persuasive message has a significant effect on attitudes. Assume further that we can identify and measure all Salient beliefs. If Fishbein's theory is correct in saying that beliefs mediate effects on attitude, we should find that statistically removing the effect of the message on beliefs (e.g., by analysis of covariance procedures) also removes the significant message effect on attitude. To the extent that the message still has significant effects on attitude, other causal processes must have occurred (or else measurement errors, etc., are present). In reality, problems arise because empirical data cannot always be interpreted as rigorous tests of the theory (see Carnegie-Mellon University Marketing Seminar 1978, Dickson and Miniard 1978 and Lutz 1978).

Perhaps the most difficult problem is demonstrating that all of the salient beliefs, and only the salient beliefs, were measured. Another problem is unambiguously demonstrating the temporal ordering of the effects. Perhaps because of these difficulties, very few studies in either psychology or marketing have addressed the validity of the basic proposition that beliefs are the sole determinant of attitudes.

Actually, Fishbein's extended model assumes that behavioural intentions are a function of both. A_{act} and a social norm construct.

Recent Research findings, however, raise the question of whether the social norm element is really a separate construct (Miniard and Cohen 1979).

Much of the marketing research based on the Fishbein model has focused on demonstrating statistically significant correlations between a "direct" measure of brand attitude (e.g. A_o) and the cognitive structure index of attitude ($\Sigma b_i e_i$) based on product attribute beliefs. Most of the studies obtained statistically significant correlations Wilkie and Pessemier 1973).

Considerable research effort has been directed at determining whether various modifications of the basic model are empirically "better" than the Fishbein formulation, even though the appropriate criteria for selecting one model over another are somewhat ambiguous. In general, this research has emphasized measurement issues and predictive validity (Lutz and Bettman 1977).

Recently, other interests related to Fishbein's attitude model have begun to emerge. Several researchers have suggested that this model provides a theoretically integrated set of measures of the cognitive effects of marketing variables particularly advertising (Mazis and Adkinson 1976, Olson and Mitchell 1975).

In applying this approach, beliefs about attributes of the advertised brand, brand attitudes, and purchase intentions are measured to indicate the multiple effects of a particular communication message on cognitive structure variables (Olson and Dover 1976).

The measures of brand attribute beliefs seem particularly useful in providing diagnostic information about the effectiveness of a message strategy.

Although, massive correlation evidence supports the static relationship between beliefs and attitudes, experimental evidence supporting the causal, mediating effect of beliefs in attitude formation and change is meagre. Manipulation of product attribute belief strengths have been demonstrated to be reflected as corresponding shifts in A_o, but relatively few marketing researchers have even included beliefs, attitudes and intentions as multiple dependent variables in the same study.

An Experimental Evaluation of *Fishbein* Theory

Mitchell and Olson (1981) examined the validity of the basic theoretical proposition of the Fishbein attitude theory. They were specifically interested in finding out whether beliefs about product attributes were the only mediators of brand attitude.

The experiment involved exposing subjects to different advertisements intended to create different brand attitudes. Because the brands were fictitious, consumers had no prior brand beliefs or attitudes. Thus, the research concerned only belief and attitude formation, not change. If Fishbein's theory is correct, the advertisements should also create differences in brand attribute beliefs. Moreover, the variation in these beliefs should account for (i.e., mediate) all the experimentally produced variation in brand attitudes.

They examined two alternatives to the beliefs-cause attitude model. Both imply that an attitude toward a concept may be formed (or changed) without the corresponding formation of salient beliefs about the concept (or changes in those beliefs). One alternative proposition suggests that sheer repetition of a stimulus may cause changes in an individual's attitude toward that stimulus.

It has been suggested that attitudes may precede beliefs in certain situations: that is, the causal flow may be reversed. Briefly stated, the notion is that attitude formation apparently can occur without belief formation under certain conditions of repeated exposure.

The other alternative proposition investigated was derived from the classical conditioning approach to attitude formation. According to this perspective, attitudes may be formed by repeatedly pairing a neutral (unconditioned) stimulus with a positively or negatively evaluated (conditioned) stimulus. For instance, an unknown brand name (UCS) could be paired in an advertisement with a picture (CS) that evokes positive feelings. The association might cause the positive feelings evoked by the picture to become conditioned to the brand name.

Both alternative propositions identify conditions under which attitudes may be formed or changed without forming or changing beliefs.

Their study was designed to create the conditions necessary to test whether brand attribute beliefs or the causal factors suggested by the alternative propositions mediate attitude formation.

They manipulated two variables -
- a) *repetition-* the number of times a particular advertisement was repeated, and
- b) *Advertising content-* whether the information presented in each ad was a verbal claim about a product attribute or merely a pairing of a brand name with one of three visual stimuli.

By repeatedly exposing subjects to different types of information, they created conditions in which attitudes could have been formed through mechanisms other than belief formation. That is, they experimentally created opportunities for a disconfirmation of the proposition that beliefs are the sole mediator of attitudes. For instance, if advertising content creates brand attitudes without parallel effects on product beliefs, such results would constitute a '"strong" disconfirmation of the beliefs-cause- attitudes proposition.

The major findings of this experiment were -
- a) There were no effects of repetition on any of the cognitive variables. Since repetition didnot appear to cause any effect on brand attitudes or beliefs, no such hypothesis as sheer repetition might directly affect attitudes but not beliefs was acceptable.

b) Advertising content manipulation had substantial multiple effects on product attribute beliefs.

c) Any mediation effect of beliefs on attitudes is due to the impact of advertising content on belief strengths and not due to any belief evaluation.

d) Manipulation of advertising content had significant effects on the strength of beliefs about several product attributes, attitudes toward the brand and attitudes toward the act of buying that brand, and purchase intentions.

e) Brand attitudes are not solely a function of the attribute beliefs that are formed about the brand, but may also be influenced by consumer's general liking for the ad itself or the visual stimulus presented in the advertisement.

f) An ad, or the overall attitude towards the advertisement, had its major mediating effect on attitudes - A_o or A_{act} i.e. overall attitude towards the brand or the attitude towards the act of buying that brand, but only a weak mediating influence on BI, i.e. behavioural intentions.

g) In this experiment, four ads. were examined only one of which contained verbal information about a product characteristic. The other three advertisements contained only visual information (Except for the brand and product names). Despite the relative lack of specific information, the belief strength measures indicate that subjects formed rather different perceptions of the four brands.

These results are of interest for several reasons. At a descriptive level they suggest that subjects, apparently by some inferential process, develop beliefs about brand attributes based on minimal brand-specific information. The results also suggest that subjects converted visual information that was not directly related to the product into meaningful semantic information.

Conclusions on *Fishbein* Theory's Testing

The experiment showed that the advertising content factor produced significant effects on three cognitive variables product attribute beliefs, attitudes and purchase intentions.

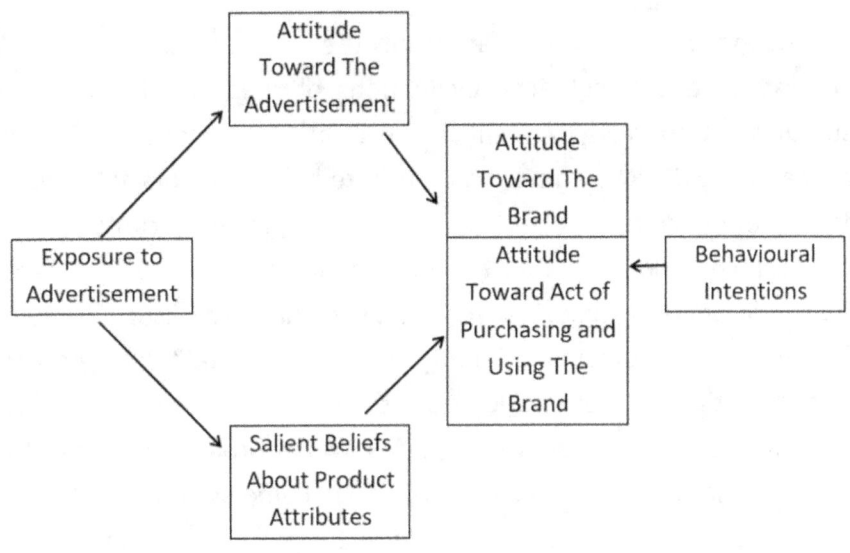

OBSERVED MEDIATORS OF ADVERTISING CONTENT ON COGNITIVE VARIABLES

Given these main effects of advertising content, the critical question is whether product attribute beliefs are the only mediator of the variation in brand attitude produced by the advertisements, or whether some other process is also operating. The mediation relationships obtained from the experiment are summarised diagrammatically above.

Do, the results obtained confirm or disconfirm Fishbein's basic proposition that beliefs cause attitude? **They seem to do both**. Although product attribute beliefs did mediate message effects on attitude as specified by Fishbein's attitude theory, such beliefs do not appear to be the only mediator. Another potential mediator, represented by the A_{ad} measure, may be operating. To understand better the meaning of these results, the A_{ad} concept calls for a closer examination.

A straightforward interpretation of the A_{ad} measure is that it accurately reflects subjects' evaluations of the overall advertising stimulus. Accordingly, A_{ad} should be treated as a construct that is conceptually distinct from brand attribute beliefs and brand attitude. Thus the mediation effect of A_{ad} can be interpreted as capturing the classical conditioning effect of pairing an unknown brand name (unconditioned stimulus) with a highly valenced visual stimulus (conditioned stimulus). In this interpretation, the conditioning process due to contiguous presentation caused the evaluation associated with the advertisement in general (A_{ad}), or with the prominent part of the advertisement such as a picture (A_{pic}), to become associated with the brand name. Presumably, this "direct" influence on attitude is independent of the message's effect on the formation of or change in product attribute beliefs. If this classical conditioning interpretation is accepted, then the information processing perspective of Fishbein is partially inconsistent with the results of this experiment.

Alternatively, one might argue that A_{ad} is a surrogate indicator or unmeasured salient beliefs about product attributes not included in the experimental questionnaire. Hence, processing the advertised information, impoverished as it was, may have created beliefs about unmeasured product attributes that somehow are reflected by the A_{ad} measure. The idea is that if the experiment had measured all the salient attribute beliefs for each subject, the A_{ad} mediation effect would not have been obtained. However, as it is not obvious how the four-item A_{ad} score could represent beliefs about unmeasured product attributes. This explanation seems somewhat strained.

Because in a general sense, beliefs are the subjective associations between cognitive representations, consumers presumably can have beliefs about any concept that they have represented cognitively. However, beliefs about the non-attribute concepts that may be associated with a brand are not measured by the typical marketing-oriented multi-attribute questionnaire. The points is that relatively little is known about the types of cognitive representations consumers may associate with a brand. Possibly, at least some of these salient beliefs do not concern traditional product attributes.

If semantic memory is conceptualized as a network of associations between cognitive representations, a set of product beliefs is a semantic memory structure. A semantic memory concept provides the basis for another explanation of the A_{ad} mediation effect.

A visual image of each advertisement is associated with the brand name representation in a consumers' memory. Such an association is conceptually equivalent to a belief. Thus, if the consumer is asked to evaluate the brand, the related visual image might be activated from memory along with other beliefs about the brand, perhaps including product attribute beliefs. If so, the evaluation of the visual image, indicated by A_{ad} in the study, should influence the overall brand attitude, A_o. By this interpretation, the A_{ad} concept is absorbed into the semantic memory structure of beliefs that are associated with the attitude concept. Thus A_{ad} is not a separate construct, but rather is a surrogate measure of $b_i e_i$; that is, A_{ad} is the evaluation of the advertisement "attribute" of the brand. If this explanation is accepted, the results are very consistent with Fishbein's proposition that beliefs cause attitude, because A_{ad} is considered another belief mediator of A_o.

The interpretation of the results of this experiment rest on the conceptual meaning of the A_{ad} construct.

In advertising effects research, for example, it may be useful to consider A_{ad} as a separate construct that can provide separate diagnostic information about an advertisement's attitudinal impact on consumers. In contrast, if the researcher is interested in memory structure, it may be more useful to consider A_{ad} as the evaluation of an image-like cognitive representation that has become associated with the brand name representation. Fishbein's attitude theory can incorporate the latter approach, but not the former.

Explanation for inferential belief formation can be given in three ways -

a) Individuals may believe that a product having a particular level of one attribute is likely to have a certain level of another attribute (Wyer 1974).

b) Memory structures for generic product categories may provide default values that enable a person to make inferences about specific attributes when information is missing (Cantor 1977, Rosch 1978).

c) The overall brand attitude may influence specific ratings of belief strength through a "halo effect" process (Mitchell 1979).

Cursors for a Different Model for Advertising Processes

The Fishbein model and the Mitchell-Olson experiment described above leads to the following pointers towards development of a new theoretical framework for advertising process -

   a) Beliefs regarding product attributes mediate brand attitudes.
   b) Brand attitudes mediate behavioural intentions.
   c) Attitude towards advertisements mediate brand attitudes.
   d) The `attitude towards advertisement' construct is not well understood, nor is its measure or causal dynamics known.
   e) Visual information is converted into semantic knowledge or beliefs about attributes of the advertised brand, and,
   f) Even seemingly irrelevant (to brand) visual stimulus go through this processing leading to formation of beliefs.

Back to Advertising as an Element of Marketing Mix

The marketing framework posits there are some people customers who have needs and they have the willingness and ability to pay for the satisfaction of those needs.

Business enterprises see an opportunity in such potential customers and design and offer products to these customers with a promise that if the customers paid for those products and consumed those products, their needs would be satisfied. The enterprise sees gains in customers paying for such offerings.

The potential customer, in the hope that consumption of the product would lead to his need-satisfaction buys the product and consumes it. The enterprise makes its gain. If the needs of the customer are satisfied, he makes his gain.

Based on the mutual perceptions of the gains made through the transaction, the business-customer interaction is sustained, grows or fades away.

Communication in general and Advertising in particular, is used as a tool by the enterprise in this interaction

    a) to inform customer that a product exists for his needs.

    b) to persuade customer that he could look forward to satisfaction of his needs through the offering

    c) to stimulate customer to buy and consume the offering

    d) to make customer realise the gains accruing to him out of this interaction

    e) to motivate customer to sustain these interactions.

However, the enterprise uses some other tools simultaneously for these interactions. It uses product design, features, attributes, packaging, branding, pricing, channels of distribution, personal selling etc. for this very purpose. So what does advertising really do and how it accomplishes it? Is advertising complementary to all such efforts or it supplements them?

In order to find answers to such questions, it is necessary to understand communications in marketing.

Communication is Perception

Communication is simply noise unless and until the audience receives it and comprehends the message embedded in it.

A receiver needs to have a concept to perceive the communication. For example, white is the colour of mourning in India but it is also the colour of the wedding gown of the bride in the west. The audience in different cultures, therefore, perceives seeing a woman in white, differently. The question is how the different audience acquired different concepts.

Well they acquired different concepts through perception. That is a circular argument - No Concept without perception, And No perception without concept. The answer lies in the fact that Perception is experience not logic, and that Perception has a range.

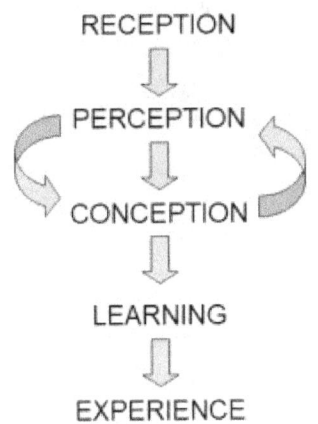

Comprehension of the message is subject to cognition (the mental action or process of acquiring knowledge and understanding through thought, experience, and the senses) of the audience. Simply put, cognition therefore, is the summation of Experience, Perception and Concept formation. Cognition is subtle. Percept and Concept are non-separable.

Receiver is the communicator because it is the receiver who controls which communication he would allow to reach him and be received by him and which he would simply block or ignore. Receiver is the communicator because he controls the comprehension of the message.

Distinction between Sanity and Paranoia is not in the ability to perceive but in the ability to learn, to change emotions based on experience. Disagreement is a result of incongruity in perceptions and not in reality. No communication can happen if there is no recipient.

Communication is Expectations

We see what we expect to see. We hear what we expect to hear. We at times resent what is unexpected. Human mind fits impressions or stimuli into a frame of expectations and attempts to 'change the mind' are resisted. Incremental changes do not help; they rather reinforce our original set of expectations.

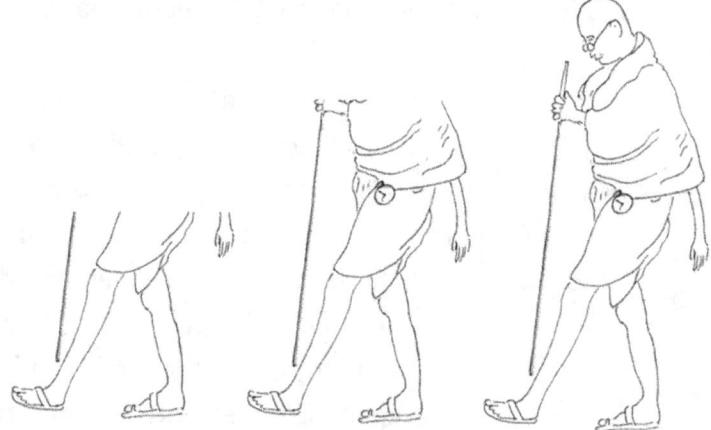

Recall this television ad where the caricature used to be formed on the screen by a swipe-up. Most Indians saw Gandhi in it because we expected to see Gandhi. Most non-Indians saw nothing more than a frugally dressed old man walking with the support of a long stick. They did not see Gandhi because they neither had the concept of a caricature of Gandhi nor the expectation of seeing him.

The Communication Process

```
                    ┌─── FEEDBACK (?) ◄───┐
                    ▼                      
    ► SENDER ············        ········► RECEIVER
    Has a message (M)   ┊                ↗ Receives it  ┄┄┐
                        └·····► MEDIA ┄┄┄                 
    ···· Encodes it ◄···┘              ┌··· Decodes it ◄··┘
    └········► Emits it ·····          └·► Perceives it (M")
                         Transmits it                ┊
                                                     ▼
    └···················· FEEDBACK (?) ◄··········· ACTIONS
```

If the communication wishes to say something different from the expectations of the recipient, there has to be a clear-cut signal that *it is different*. Recipient needs to be forced to realise that the unexpected is happening.

Communication is Involvement

Communication is not information, though it may have information embedded in it. It is possible to have communication between the sender and the receiver with nil information, but information cannot be transmitted without communication between the sender and the receiver.

Information is pure logic. History is communication but not information. Communications is not mere transmitting of information; it has an emotional charge. It makes demands from the recipient to:
- Become somebody
- Do something
- Believe something

Irrelevant makes no emotional demand. Communication that fits into Aspirations, Values and Purpose of the recipient is powerful.

Propaganda (communication where the source of the message is unknown) is very powerful in the short-run. However, over a period, it is a waste. A number of techniques based on social psychological research are used to generate propaganda. Propagandists use arguments that, while sometimes convincing, are not necessarily valid. Marketing involves persuasive communication between the seller (sender) and the buyer (recipient) to move the buyer towards buying. Promotion is the aggregate of persuasive communication of which advertising is a more visible and possibly bigger chunk of effort.

COMMUNICATION AS PART OF PROMOTION

Marketing Forces (Moving people towards buying)

- ADVERTISING
- PROMOTIONS
- PERSONAL SELLING
- PUBLICITY
- USER RECOMMENDATIONS
- AVAILABILITY
- DISPLAY
- PRICE
- PACKAGING
- EXHIBITS

Stages: Unawareness → Awareness → Comprehension → Conviction → Action

Countervailing Forces:
- COMPETITION
- MEMORY LAPSES
- SALES RESISTANCE
- MARKET ATTRITION (deaths, relocations)

Communication in marketing would not exist without a suitable recipient. It is imperative therefore to analyse the buying process in terms of understanding:

Who is the decision-making unit? Who is the -
- Initiator of purchase
- Influencer (opinion leader) of purchase
- Decider of purchase
- Purchaser
- User

What is the decision making process? In terms of its-
- Scope and timing
- Perceptions and criteria
- Perceived risk (type of "buy")
- Brand loyalty vs. price sensitivity
- Information needs

Purchase characteristics, in terms of -
- Who makes the purchase?
- Why does he make the purchase?
- Where does he make the purchase?
- When does he make the purchase?
- How often does he make the purchase?

Communication Relevant Theories

• *Constructivism*: Theory that focuses on the ability to differentiate the way people make sense of things (i.e., personal constructs) and to create person-cantered messages.

• *Cognitive-Behavioural Theory*: Theory suggesting that the way individuals construe or interpret events and situations mediates how they subsequently feel and behave. Communication is used to disconfirm irrational beliefs and to teach strategies for change, including cognitive restructuring.

- *Social Judgment Theory*: Theory postulating that people respond to communication with a latitude of acceptance, rejection, or non-commitment. Depending on ego-involvement (i.e., how important an issue is to them), people can be influenced along a certain latitude.

- *Elaboration Likelihood Model*: Theory indicating that people respond to messages along one of two paths: the elaboration (i.e., central) path or the peripheral path. The elaboration path is associated with reflectively thinking about, internalizing, and processing information in a fair and objective manner. Most messages are processed via the peripheral route in an effort to avoid information overload. This pathway is not associated with long-term program success.

- *The Extended Parallel Process Model*: A fear appeal theory postulating that threat motivates action, (e.g., too much unprotected exposure to the sun causes skin cancer) and that perceived efficacy (i.e., confidence in one's ability to take recommended action) determines whether the recommended action taken (e.g., wearing a hat or using sunscreen when in the sun) controls the danger or controls the fear (e.g., getting skin cancer). For communication purposes, it is important that high efficacy messages (e.g., sun screen is easy to obtain and apply) accompany high threat messages (e.g., one needs to avoid skin cancer).

- *The Spiral of Silence*: Theory indicating that the fear of isolation causes people to remain silent about minority opinions and even adopt the majority opinion despite personal and philosophical concerns. The mass media may perpetuate this repression of views through constant repetition or coverage of certain themes.

- *Theory of Reasoned Action*: Theory asserting that behaviour is predicted by intentions related to the behaviour. These intentions are in turn predicted by attitudes toward the behaviour and by subjective norms. Subjective norms are predicted by normative beliefs and the motivation to comply with those normative beliefs. Persuasive communication should target the audience's salient beliefs about the consequences of performing a certain behaviour and the audience's attitudes toward those consequences. To persuade, communication should also address the audience's beliefs about what other people think about the behaviour and the audience's motivation to comply with the perceived beliefs of others (i.e., to adopt the subjective norm).

• *The Agenda-Setting Function*: Theory suggesting that the mass media strongly influence and shape people's thoughts and the priorities they develop. For example, if a specific health problem receives constant attention in the media, the population may soon believe through association that the health problem is an important one.

• *Cultivation Theory*: Theory indicating that television has become a primary source of information. What people see on television, particularly with respect to violence, cultivates a distorted view of reality and builds exaggerated social norms.

• *Stages of Change Model*: Theory postulating that behaviour is a process and not an event. Individuals are at varying levels of motivation or readiness to change. People at different points in the process of change can benefit from different interventions matched to their stage at the time.

• *Health Belief Model*: Theory relating to how individuals perceive the threat of a health problem and appraise recommended behaviours for preventing or managing the problem.

• *Consumer Information Processing Model*: Theory of how individuals (i.e., consumers) acquire and use information in their decision-making.

- *Social Learning Theory*: Theory indicating that people learn not only from their own experiences, but also by observing the actions of others and the consequences of those actions (i.e., modelling).

- *Community Organization Theories*: Theories suggesting that as problem solving skills of a community are enhanced through locality development, social planning, and social action; the community is empowered to achieve concrete change to redress social injustice. • Organizational Change Theory: Theory that includes processes and strategies for increasing the chances that health policies and programs will be adopted and maintained in formal organizations.

- *Diffusion of Innovations Theory*: Theory addressing how new ideas, products, and social practices are spread within a community or from one community to another.

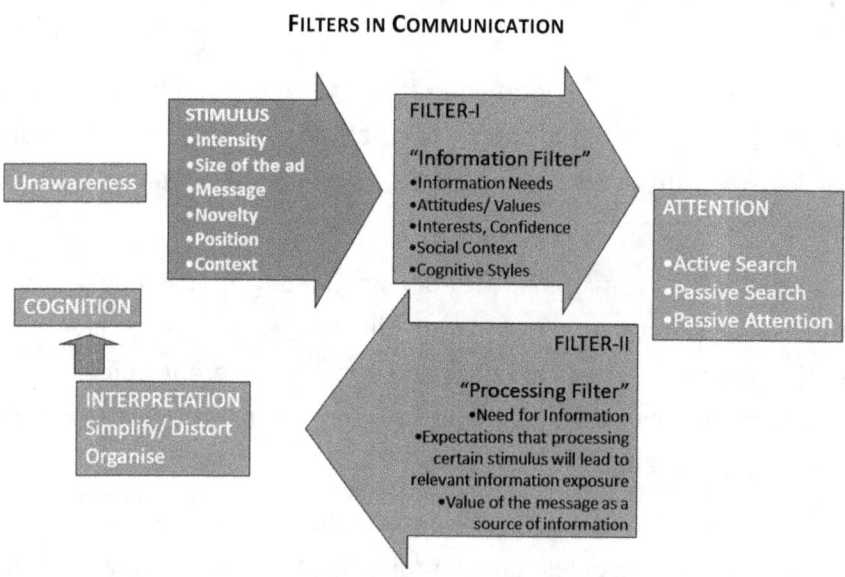

FILTERS IN COMMUNICATION

The recipient by choice and because of his limitations may not receive the message as it was sent. There could be distortions.

Response Hierarchy Models

Since, we are concerned with the desired response to communication, a comparison is made for finding out correspondence amongst steps of hierarchy among the three most universally adopted hierarchies of communication.

The American businessperson, E. St. Elmo Lewis, developed the *AIDA model* in 1898. The original main purpose was to optimize sales calls, specifically the interaction between seller and buyer concerning the product. Lewis can be considered a pioneer when it comes to the use of scientific methods for designing advertising and sales processes. At the same time, it was very important for Lewis to view advertising as a type of "training" that assisted the beneficiary. Lewis's theoretical explanations of advertising theory rested on extensive experience.

RESPONSE HIERARCHY MODELS

Stage	AIDA	Hierarchy of Effects	Innovation Adoption	Communications
Cognitive Stage	Attention	Awareness ↓ Knowledge	Awareness	Exposure ↓ Reception ↓ Cognition
Affective Stage	Interest ↓ Desire	Liking ↓ Preference ↓ Conviction	Interest ↓ Evaluation ↓ Trial	Attitude ↓ Intention
Behaviour Stage	Action	Purchase	Adoption	Behaviour

The *Hierarchy of Effects Model* was created in 1961 by Robert J Lavidge and Gary A Steiner. This marketing communication model, suggests there are six steps from viewing a product advertisement (advert) to product purchase. The job of the advertiser is to encourage the customer to go through the six steps and purchase the product. This hierarchy is conceptualised as a causal chain of links between proximal variables and endpoints or distal outcomes.

Diffusion of Innovation (DOI) Theory, developed by E.M. Rogers in 1962, is one of the oldest social science theories. It originated in communication to explain how, over time, an idea or product gains momentum and diffuses (or spreads) through a specific population or social system. The result of this diffusion is that people, as part of a social system, adopt a new idea, behaviour, or product. Adoption means that a person does something differently than what they had previously (i.e., purchase or use a new product, acquire and perform a new behaviour, etc.). The key to adoption is that the person must perceive the idea, behaviour, or product as new or innovative. It is through this that diffusion is possible.

A Fresh Take on Advertising Effects

Repeated attempts to find failure of Response Hierarchy Effects have failed. Yet, there are no conclusive evidence of such theories being valid. It is for this reason that even after 60 years of their existence, they continue to be theories rather than principles.

A recurring problem for marketing communication planners is the nature of the hierarchy of communication effects. Does awareness lead to comprehension to conviction and then to purchasing behaviour? It depends. In fact three kinds of hierarchies are now accepted: the standard Learning ones mentioned above, the Dissonance-Attribution hierarchy in which action occurs first, then attitude shift and finally awareness and comprehension, and the Low-

Involvement hierarchy originally developed by Herbert E. Krugman. For low-involvement situations, awareness and minimal comprehension occurs first, then purchasing action and finally attitude or conviction change. Briefly, the standard Learning hierarchy seems to occur when buyers are involved, alternative products are clearly differentiated, mass media promotion is important and the product is in the early stages of the product life cycle. The Dissonance-Attribution hierarchy--with purchasing action first-- seems to occur when buyers are involved, products are similar, personal selling is more important, and the product is in the early maturity stage of its life cycle. The Krugman Low-Involvement hierarchy occurs when involvement is low, products are seen as similar, broadcast media are important, and the product is in late maturity.

STAGE SKIPPING IN DISSONANCE-ATTRIBUTION AND LOW-INVOLVEMENT MODELS

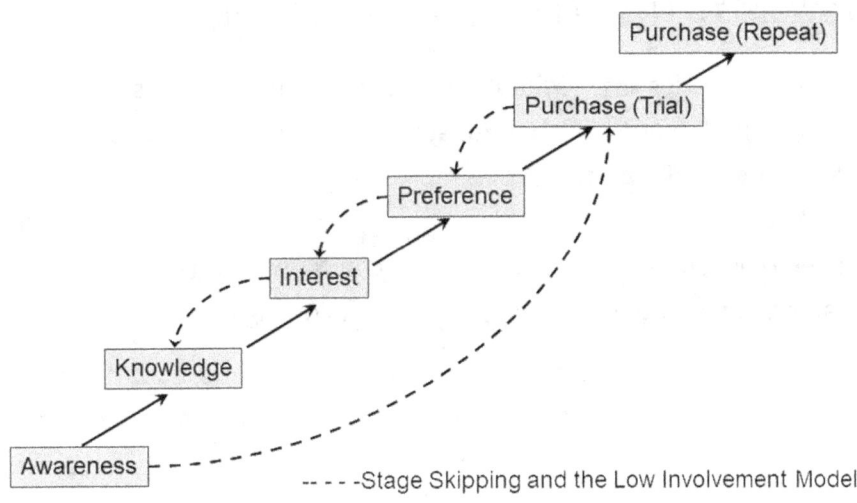

- - - - Stage Skipping and the Low Involvement Model

Since the unit of interaction between the enterprise and the customer is an exchange of product for a price, what is the framework for exchange? This is to say -

a) What are the conditions necessary for an exchange to take place?
b) What are the conditions sufficient for the exchange to take place?
c) Under what conditions would the exchange be repeated?
d) When would the exchange not get repeated?
e) Can a sustained exchange get disrupted? If yes, under what conditions?
f) How can another exchange take place when the outcome of earlier exchange ruled out a repeat exchange?
g) What is the role of advertising in exchange process?
h) How does this role change in the various exchange situations listed above?

Towards a New Theory of Advertising

We have theories, lots of them. None of them seems to be satisfactory enough though none of them unacceptable. This may call for a fresh perspective and may be yet one more theory.

Advertising should be viewed as a communication in marketing. Marketing communication works on the following basis:

a) Each human being has some beliefs about oneself. These beliefs are shaped out of ones experience, knowledge, learning, surroundings, society and culture. This leads to some kind of an image that one has about oneself. This is termed as *Self Image*.

b) Each person, when one comes across a brand, be it through display, advertising, usage, thrown away package, its mention from someone else, etc. starts developing beliefs about that brand. These beliefs together work to create a mental picture of that brand in the mind of the person that is much wider than just a photo-picture. This image is called as *Brand Image*.

c) When the brand comes for consideration of buying and acquisition, the questions that come to the mind of the potential customer include, among other things, issues like where is this brand sold, who is the manufacturer or marketer of the brand, what kind of organisation they are, and so on. These could be already known or new organisations. Again, the person uses ones experience, knowledge, learning, surroundings, location, stocking patterns etc. to form images about the source of supply for the product. This image is called the *Source Image*.

d) The three images are independent of each other in the mental space of the audience. This is to say that they are orthogonal.

e) The entire gambit of customers' response to marketing programmes of an organisation has to relate to these three images, viz., *Brand Image, Self Image* and *Source Image*.

f) When the customer finds some kind of a congruence between the three images, they get favourable disposed towards the brand which may lead to typical responses like recognition, recall, trial, repeat or brand loyalties. Conversely, lack of congruence in images could result in lack of such responses.

g) Marketing communications affect the beliefs that people have for brands. Through its persuasive appeals to the psyche of the audience, they shape beliefs that people have about themselves. Marketing communications inform people about the source of the products and what that source stands for. Beliefs about the source are thus shaped. It amounts to saying that advertising shapes the three images, *Brand Image*, *Self Image* and *Source Image*.

IMAGE CONGRUENCE MODEL OF ADVERTISING

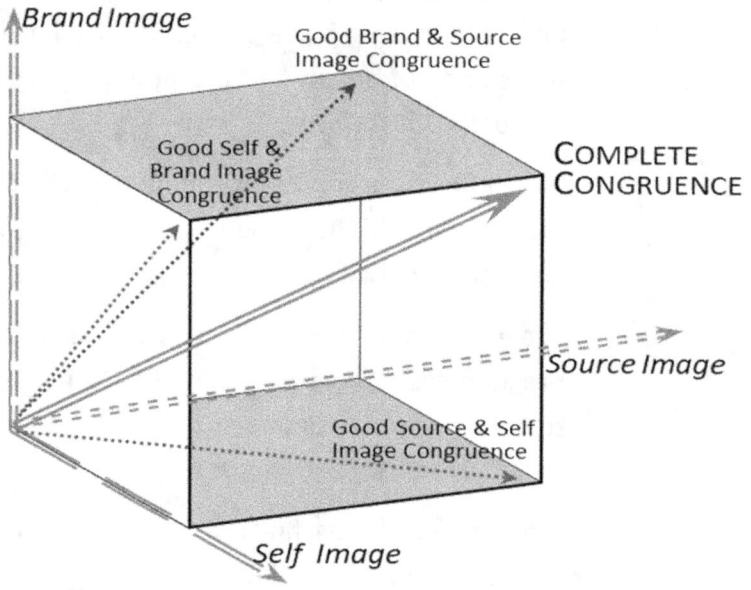

h) Since these beliefs and images are shaped not just by advertising but also by all other stimuli, advertising works one-step further. It creates or attempts to create some kind of a congruence in these three images in the minds of its audience.

i) Congruence in *all images lead to sales effects*. Congruence in BRAND IMAGE and SELF IMAGE lead to recall and attitudes but poor sales. Congruence in SELF IMAGE and SOURCE IMAGE leads to inquiries and trials; and so on.

j) Advertising works through image congruence. Extent of congruence results in varying advertising effects.

Testing the New Theory

The above theory could be simply stated in terms of the following hypothesis, which could be subjected to testing:

H_1 : Every customer has a perception about himself that is referred to as personal image.

H_2 : This perception of his own image is closer to his perceptions of an ideal person rather than his real self.

H_3 : Customer ascribes a person like imagery to every product that he knows of or comes to know of at any point of time. The dimension of such imagery are aggregated as product image.

H_4 : Customer also ascribes a person type image to the place where an exchange could take place. This place may include the shop, seller, or seller's agent.

H_5 : An exchange takes place when the three images are congruent or match with each other.

H_6 : Advertising shapes the customers' perceptions on product image and place image.

H_7 : Advertising shapes even the perceptions of one's own image.

H_8 : Advertising matches the three images that results in an exchange.

H_9 : Mismatch in images leads to rupture in enterprise-customer exchange.

H_{10} : Advertising can lead to a mismatch in images as well as cause a matching in the mismatched images.

If the above hypotheses are not rejected, it would be possible to accept the above theory for advertising. The process of testing of these hypotheses could help create some standard research instrument subsequently which could be used as a standard tool to pre-test advertising campaigns rather than advertisements.

The Methodology to Test

The theory was put subjected to testing through a customer survey carried out to make measurements and testing of various hypothesis listed above. This was the subject matter of doctoral dissertation of the author.

Since cause and effect relationships were studied, a conclusive research design was used. While no research in social sciences can provide an absolute proof for causation, efforts were made to develop a design that approaches a high degree of causal connection as an entirely new way of explaining advertising effects was proposed. In spite of best efforts, one would still need to view these measurements as a probable relationship rather than with complete certainty.

Image measurements were made using the VALS-2 inventory, suitably adapted. Data was collected using a structured, self-administered questionnaire. The questionnaire was repeatedly pre-tested and modified. A multi-stage sampling method was used for this study; the stages being – 2 cities selected by convenience, each divided into clusters as designated by local pin codes, two cluster from each city selected using the random process through SPSS, using quota control based on gender and age-groups for picking up the respondent household, the last stage being snow-ball sampling.

Since the classification data for the respondents was obtained both for Occupation as well as Highest Education attained by the head of the family, it was possible to use the cross-tabulation to label the respondents according to their SEC class. VALS-2 data was subjected to Factor Analysis followed by Clustering of Factor Scores to arrive at three types of self-image. Brands bought, Brands not bought, stores bought from and stores not bought from were all clustered into three classes each. Thus, we had at least three classes of imagery for all three images, self, brand and source. Correlations were then run between self-image, brand image and source image cluster memberships. To validate, multidimensional scaling using Euclidean distance measures for similarities was attempted.

According to this test, advertising works on the following basis:

1. The entire gambit of customers' response to marketing programmes of an organisation has to relate to the three images, viz., Brand Image, Self-Image and Source Image.

2. When the customer finds some kind of congruence among the three images, they get favourably disposed towards the brand that may lead to typical responses like recognition, recall, trial, repeat or brand loyalties. Conversely, lack of congruence in images could result in lack of such responses.

3. Advertising shapes the three images; Brand Image, Self-Image and Source Image, and then creates or attempts to create some kind of congruence in these three images in the minds of its audience.

4. Advertising works through image shaping and image congruence. Extent of congruence results in varying advertising effects.

The uses of this model can be immediately seen in-

- Communication strategy formulation and evaluation
- Advertising effectiveness studies
- pre-testing of advertising rather than advertisements, and
- Marketing strategy formulation and evaluation.

Like all projects, this work should also end somewhere. The discussions reported above only illustrates the extent of ignorance one has towards the institution of advertising. The Motivation to carry on the work of theory building is obviously there. That would need to wait for some other time.

5

Planning the Persuasive Communication♠

In order to achieve their objectives, business entities have an overall strategy, called the corporate strategy, execution of which is expected to deliver the results commensurate with the defined milestones and goal posts. Such strategy devolves to the functional areas like manufacturing, finance, logistics, people-management or marketing as their individualised milestones and goal posts.

Down the Ladder of Goals, Strategies and Toolkits

These functional areas hence design their functional strategies, which are sub-strategies within the overall corporate strategy. Marketing function therefore has a marketing strategy. Implementation of such

---

♠ A plethora of books on the topic of this chapter and the succeeding one, many of them very popular, others less popular, few from illustrious practitioners of the craft of advertising, many from the obscure ones, are already in the libraries and on the www, few of them decorating the office shelves of academics and advertising managers. More keep tricking in every year in the character of textbooks from academic authors, most of whom have never ever written an advertising brief or seen the production of advertising. No one is missing or waiting for another book on the topic. These two chapters have therefore been contained in less than 70 small size pages instead of the usual 700 large size ones. ***Brevity is the soul of wit and wisdom.***

marketing strategy by the marketing managers is accomplished through a toolkit generally known as the marketing-mix.

Marketing managers choose a combination of different tools from the toolkit in performing their tasks. They can use the tools as multipliers, supplements, substitutes or compliments of one another depending on their wisdom, acumen, knowledge and assessment of the requirements.

Promotion is persuasive communication, a tool that has a set of small driver-heads more suited to different audiences and different contexts. This set of driver-heads of promotion is called the promotion-mix. Sales-Promotion is a short-term inducement directed at the consumer or the channel partners or the sales force. Personal selling is a one to one or one to many bilateral communication between the seller and the customer in real-time, although it could be carried on face-to-face or over audio or video calling.

THE MARKETING MIX

Advertising is the communication to absent audience. This is so, for the reason that the advertisement is created by the sender and handed over to the medium. No audience is present when the advertisement is created or handed over to the medium. The medium delivers it to its audience. When the audience receives the message, the sender is nowhere in sight. The audience is able to discern between the editorial content of the medium and the advertiser's message. The medium assists the audience in making such distinction.

Publicity is not Advertising, PR is not Publicity

Publicity is the placement of the message in the editorial space of the medium. The audience is unable to discern between the editorial content of the medium and the advertiser's message. The medium does not want the audience to be able to make such a distinction. Such messaging may have higher credibility but lower creative control of the sender.

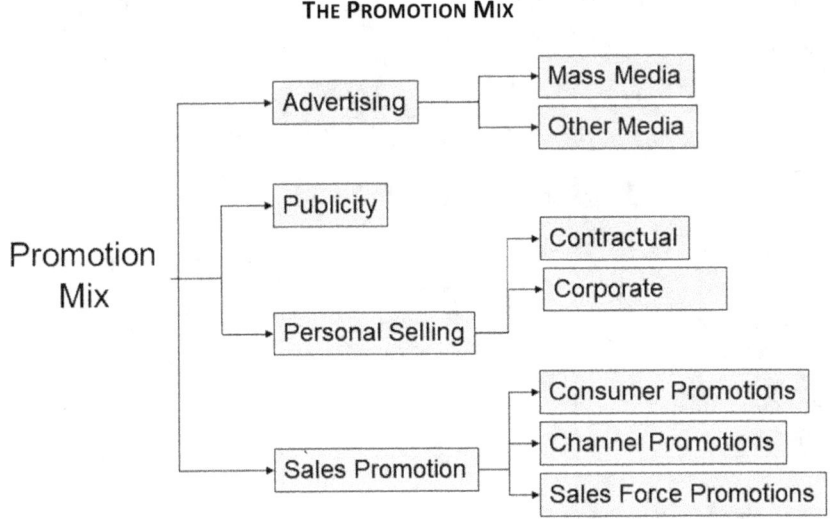

THE PROMOTION MIX

For reasons of magniloquence, promotion in general and advertising in particular is confused and interchangeably used with a term *'public-relations.'*

Public Relations is a completely different function from marketing. Public relations is about managing the relationship of business entity with its stakeholders and publics. While stakeholders, both internal and external are directly affected by the performance of business entity, publics are other bodies or individuals who do not have any direct stake in the business entity but are deeply interested in the affairs of the business entity for their non-proximate impact on the interests of such bodies or individuals. Such publics have similar interests in the affairs of many business entities, and are often able to influence public opinion and political opinion, two of the tools in the marketing-mix.

While the public relations' tool-kit is not identical to the marketing-tool-kit, both the toolkits have a few identical tools, advertising being one of them.

PUBLIC RELATIONS

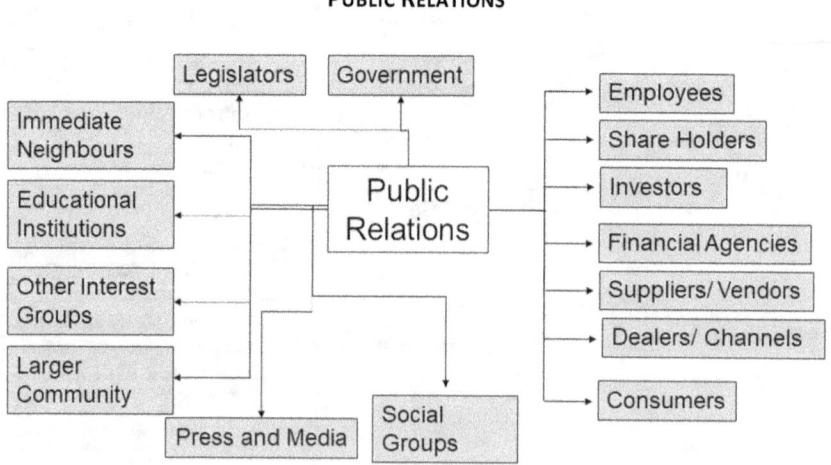

Corporate advertising is one that is directed towards consumers and publics together. Similarly, consumers in their lives perform roles, which put them into one or the other publics. Consumers could simultaneously be investors, suppliers, employees or legislators.

Such multiplicity of roles of consumers as publics and similarity of communication-tools deployed in reaching out to the consumers and the publics causes the confusion leading to the slip-up of treating advertising as the same as public relations. It is however pertinent to differentiate between them for designing appropriate strategy and delivering proper implementation. In the two cases, the messages are different and the response desired of the audience is different.

Cheat-sheet for Marketing Communications

MarCom is not just advertising and personal selling, but also:

- Sales promotion
- Trade promotion and
- Consumer promotion
- Direct Mail, Trade Shows
- Point of sale material, Packaging

Even:
- Pricing
- Distribution channels, and
- Word of mouth

What Can Advertising Do?

- Position the product
- Create an image

- Provide reassurance
- Introduce new products
- Give specifications
- Provide use ideas
- Tell where to buy
- Establish brand awareness and package familiarity
- Develop retailer interest
- Build internal morale; set performance standards

Advertising Is Especially Appropriate when:

- Mass media can convey the message
- Product can be positioned psycho-graphically
- Sales volume base can support the cost
- Brand loyalty is relatively low: consumers are willing to switch

What Can Personal Selling Do?

- Identify prospective customers
- Develop tailored solutions
- Reassure buyers
- Gather vital feedback on
- New opportunities
- Product performance
- Competitive activity
- Market demand
- Handle customer problems
- Product failures
- Late deliveries
- Shortages
- Excess stock

Personal Selling Is Especially Useful When:

- Customers want to see the product
- Tailored solutions are needed
- Mass media can't target the customers
- Mass media can't effectively convey the message

Sales Promotion Can:

- Reinforce ad message at point-of-sale
- Trigger impulse buying
- Generate consumer excitement
- Stimulate brand switching
- And Is Especially Useful:
- In highly competitive markets
- For attracting in-store attention
- For low-risk purchases

Marketing Communications Programme

It all begins with the analysis of competition.

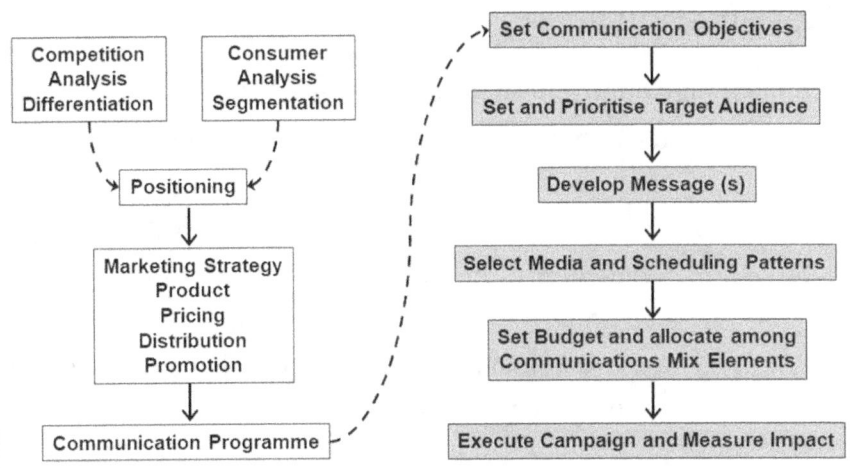

This analysis brings out points-of-parity and points-of-differentiation between products and brands.

Simultaneously, analysis of consumer buying provides bases for segmentation. Most of this analysis is an overlap between marketing and communications as it trickles down for a more general marketing approach to a more specific communication approach.

Objectives in developing a segmentation strategy

Identify a group of consumers that –
- Are not being served well presently by competition, and
- Are large enough, or growing in size; and
- Are most likely to respond positively to the benefits offered by our brand.

Segment to DIFFERENTIATE and TARGET
- no need to segment if the marketing approach or strategy is going to be undifferentiated

Segmentation and Positioning

Since all potential customers are not identical –
- DIFFERENTIATION – Focus on two or more sub-groups through different marketing programmes
- CONCENTRATION – Focus on only one sub-group and develop one programme tailored to just that single sub-group
- UNDIFFERENTIATING or AGGREGATION – One programme for all sub-groups

Cautions in Segmentation

- A segment with large potential may not be the most profitable (Majority Fallacy)
- Concentration in very large segments may be un-differentiation and in very small segments – a NICHE
- Segmentation is not always the most optimal approach

"Generally" –
> As a product-class gains maturity, consumer needs often become more specialised and segmentation strategy is a natural response of manufacturers to these needs.

Approaches to Segmentation

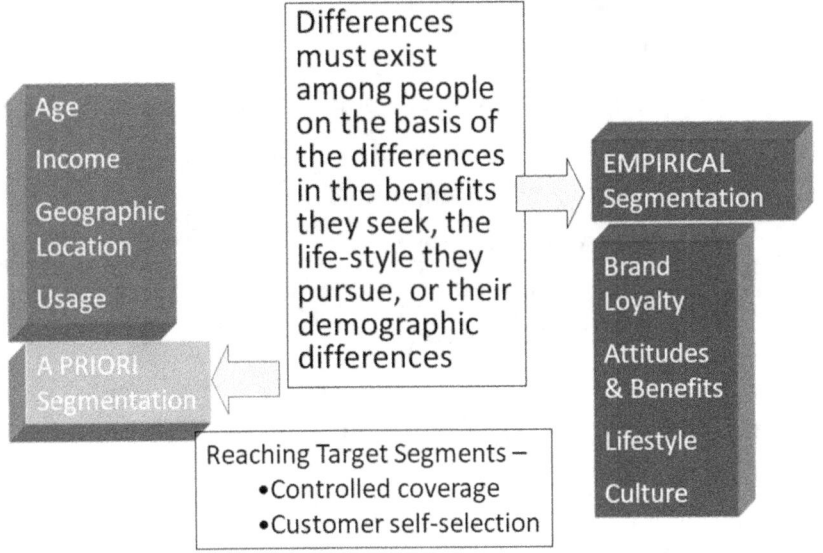

Implementing a Segmentation Strategy

- Develop and position products/ services for particular segments

- Select distribution channels to reach certain groups
- Design pricing to attract particular type of buyers
- Advertise to appeal to certain types of customers

Positioning Strategy

- Using Product Characteristics or Customer Benefits
- Price – Quality Approach
- Use or Application Approach
- Product – User Approach
- Cultural Symbol Approach
- Competitor Approach

Determining the Positioning Strategy

- Identify the Competitor
- Determine how the competitors are perceived and evaluated
- Determine the competitors' position
- Analyse the customer
- Select the position
- Monitor the position

Setting Objectives for Advertising

Advertising Goals

- Explicit Statement of Advertising Goals
- Why these Advertising Goals have been selected

Advertising Strategies

- Advertising Creative Strategies

- The recommended strategy and reasons for recommendation
- Alternative Strategies Considered
* Advertising Media Strategies
  - The recommended strategy and reasons for recommendation.
  - Alternative Strategies Considered

Advertising Tactics

* Creative Tactics.
  - Recommended advertising and reasons thereof
  - Relation of recommended advertising to creative strategy
  - Alternative advertising; why alternatives are ignored
* Media Tactics
  - Recommended media plan and reasons for recommendation
  - Relation of recommended media plan to media strategy
  - Alternative media plans; why alternatives are not recommended (optional)
* Advertising Market Tests, if any
  - Tests of Advertising Budget Levels Planned
  - Tests of Alternative Creative Strategies and Tactics
  - Tests of Alternative Media Strategies and Tactics
* Advertising Effectiveness Research

DAGMAR was the study of Association of National Advertisers (ANA) that the goal of advertising is to achieve specialized objectives and it recognized that different advertisements could have a number of objectives. Russel H. Colley, an economist carried out the study, who stated, "*Advertising's job, purely and. simply, is to communicate to a defined audience information and a frame of mind that stimulates action. Advertising succeeds or fails, depending on how well it communicates the desired information and attitudes to the right people at the right time and at the right cost.*"

DAGMAR Approach

- DEFINING ADVERTISING GOALS FOR MEASURED ADVERTISING RESULTS – by Russell H Colley
    - To what extent does the advertising aim at closing an immediate sale?
    - Does the advertising aim at near-term sales by moving the prospect, step by step, closer to a sale?
    - Build familiarity and easy recognition of package or trademark
    - Specifically, how can advertising contribute towards increased sales?
    - Does the advertising aim at some specific step which leads to sale?
    - How important are "Supplementary Benefits" of end-use advertising?
    - Is it a task of advertising to impart information needed to consummate sales and build customer satisfaction?
    - To what extent does the advertising aim at building confidence and goodwill for the corporation?
    - Specifically what kind of image does the company wish to build?

Colley was very specific as to the levels of hierarchy of communication effects – *unawareness, awareness, comprehension, conviction, action,* and their relationship over time in response to advertising effort.

Usual Goals for Advertisers – by their type

For Direct-Response Advertiser
- Order, coupons, inquiry, donations, etc.

For Retail Advertiser
- Continuous retailing but sporadic advertising
- Goals in terms of advertising and incremental sales

For Packaged Goods Advertiser
- Goals in terms of brand switch or market share, or, also, total sales or time taken to recoup ad expenditure

For other advertised goods and services
- Establish a model of specific effects that advertising has to create alongside other elements of marketing mix

Brand Personality

Brands may be characterised as (bipolar)–
- Adventurous
- Head-strong
- Undependable
- Excitable, or
- Somewhat crude

Why is Brand Personality important?
When is Brand personality more important?

Executing a Brand Personality Strategy-

- Endorser (vs. Advocacy)
- User Imagery
- Creative Execution Elements
- Consistency

Benefits Based Attitudes

Once the target market is identified, the positioning and Communication objectives set, decision must be made about the content of the advertising message (message strategy).

What should the message focus on –

- Communicating product benefits
- Developing/ reinforcing brand image or personality
- Evoking special feelings or emotions
- Developing group associations

Benefits are characteristics or attributes of a product that consumers perceive positively. Issue is –

- Which and how many of them to focus on in an advertising campaign?
- Are product attributes and images linked to overall attitudes of consumers?
- Do perceptions, feelings and beliefs influence the decision process?

Components of Attitudes are –

- Cognitive
- Affective
- Co-native

While Attributes are made up of –

- Physical characteristics
- Pseudo-physical characteristics
- Benefits

Identifying important attributes is done through -
- Rating
- Ranking
- Conjoint-analysis

Issue is –
- which and how many of them to focus on in an advertising campaign?
- Are product attributes and images linked to overall attitudes of consumers?
- Do perceptions, feelings and beliefs influence the decision process?
- What are Leverage and Determinant attributes, which ones to use, and how to use them?

Associating Feelings with Brands

- Feelings such as warmth, happiness or fear can be associated with brands and can influence attitudes and behaviour towards the brand
- Positive moods can increase positive thoughts and brand attitudes may be formed an ad-likeability rather than intrinsic product quality
- Transformation of experience in use by associating feelings with it. Thus, quality of experience is enhanced.
- Ads may be liked because they are enjoyable and they are informative & useful. When a feeling-based ad leads to a more positive attitude towards the ad, it can lead to more positive brand attitudes.
- A good feeling is associated with the ad, the ad is then associated with the brand.

- Later exposure to the brand even without the ad stimulates the same feeling response.

Product Advertising usually focusses on

- Familiarity
- Announcement and Information
- Differentiation
- Positioning
- Brand-Customer connect
- Brand-consumer connect

Corporate Advertising is usually undertaken for

- *Corporate Identity* -Reinforce Identity or reputation
- *Financial* - Solicit Investor Interest – Raise Capital
- *Advocacy* - Influence Public Opinion

Developing a Communication Brief

A communication brief is the document that lays down the terms of reference from the client to the agency. The client may prepare the brief and the agency may get it amended, since communication strategy development and advertising planning is a joint activity. The brief is *founded in Research*, which is undertaken in the three phases of the advertising planning process -

- Strategy generation
- Creative development
- Campaign evaluation

The brief contains the *Consumer Insight*, which intersects with the interests of the customer, and the brand features. Insights are not easy to come by, they are to be mined, by the client or the agency or both to ascertain, with respect to the *Desired Response* from the audience-

- Realistic response objective?
- Causes of non-response?
- Barriers to desired response?
- Motivation to respond?
- Role of each element in the communication mix

The brief explains the consumer insight and summarizes the basic strategy decisions. Invariably, a communication brief has *six major parts*:

- Marketing objective
- Product
- Target audience
- The promise and support
- Brand personality
- Strategy statement

The essential questions in a creative brief are –

- "Who are we talking to?"
- "why?", and
- "What do we want to say?"

Advertising Appropriations and Budgets

Two fundamental Questions:

- How much to spend?
- How to spend that much?

Theory and Literature does not help in answering these questions. No consensus amongst practitioners regarding what method to use

Modelling Relationships between Advertising Expenditures, Sales and Profits

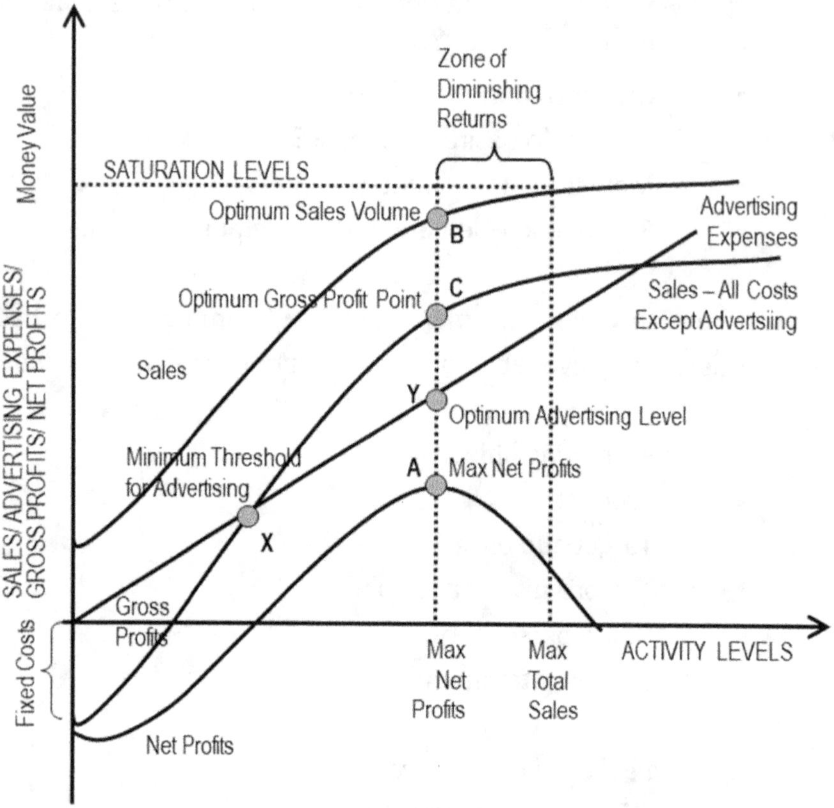

Usual Approaches

- Percentage of Sales or Unit of Sales
- Increase over past year
- Competitive Parity
- Objective and Task
- Capital Budgeting
- Others
    - Affordability
    - Arbitrary
    - Modelling

Attention is a necessary ingredient for effective advertising. The market for consumer attention (or "eyeballs") has become so competitive that attention can be regarded as a currency. The rising cost of this ingredient in the marketplace is causing marketers to waste money on costly attention sources or reduce their investment in promoting their brands. Instead, they should be thinking about how to "buy" cheaper attention and how to use it more effectively.

Strategy of Advertising

With the increasing usage of digital media by consumers, more companies are using digital marketing to reach their target markets.

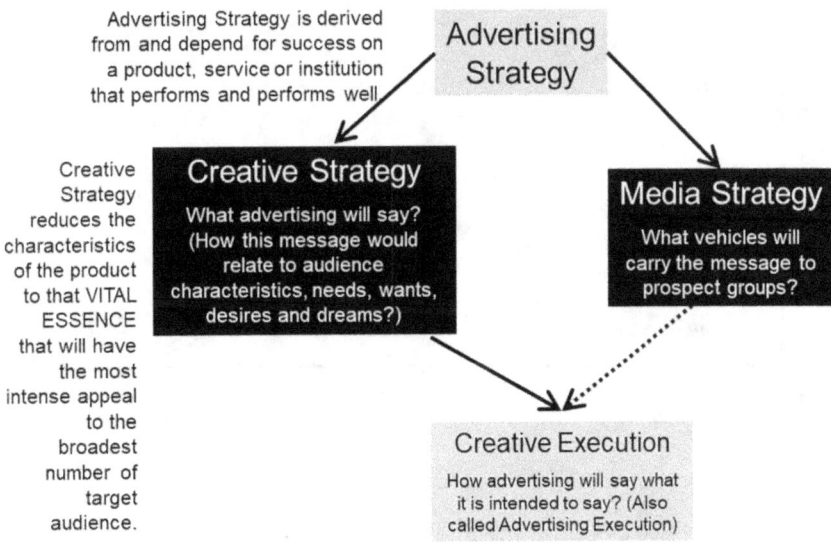

It is prudent to note that emergence of new media forms or changes in media-consumption habits of the consumer does not change the strategy in advertising. Such changes influence the tactical decisions related to media-class, media-vehicle, media-options and scheduling/timing of release of advertising.

The market is cluttered with context-based strategy books like – digital advertising, social-media advertising, e-marketing, marketing in the virtual world, online advertising and so on.

Of the Latest Gartner Hype Cycles for Digital Marketing and Advertising presented at the site, **https://www.smartinsights.com/managing-digital-marketing/marketing-innovation/technology-for-innovation-in-marketing/** the most interesting graphic from Gartner is below:

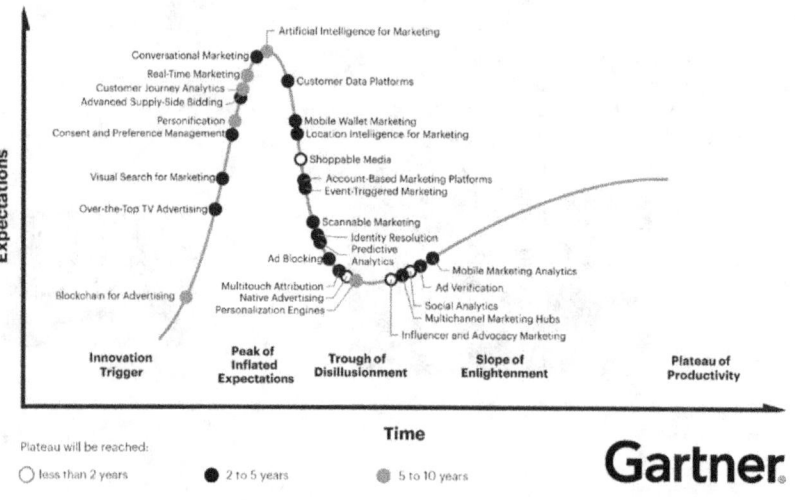

The fundamentals of strategy in advertising have not changed.

6

Creating and Delivering Advertisements♥

>MEN WANTED.
>LOW WAGE. BITTER COLD.
>LONG MONTHS OF DARKNESS.
>UNDER CONSTANT DANGER.
>SAFE RETURN DOUBTFUL.
>HONOUR AND RECOGNITION IF SUCCESSFUL.

This ad in a London daily for a polar expedition in 1941 brought over 5000 applications.

Simply put, advertising is the act of persuasive messaging through a means of communication, indulged into by the advertiser, with the intention of seeking a desired response from a target audience.

♥ A plethora of books on the topic of this chapter and the preceding one, many of them very popular, others less popular, few from illustrious practitioners of the craft of advertising, many from the obscure ones, are already in the libraries and on the www, few of them decorating the office shelves of academics and advertising managers. More keep tricking in every year in the character of textbooks from academic authors, most of whom have never ever written an advertising brief or seen the production of advertising. No one is missing or waiting for another book on the topic. These two chapters have therefore been contained in less than 70 small size pages instead of the usual 700 large size ones. **Brevity is the soul of wit and wisdom.**

Thus, there is a message, there is a medium (messenger), there is a sender of the message and there is a recipient of the message. The message intends to persuade the recipient to respond to the message in a form and way, which the sender desires.

Advertisement is the message packaged in a way so that the messenger (medium) could carry it to the intended recipient, on behalf of the sender. The packaging of the message is therefore in the form of a print, note, sound, pictures – could be still or moving, audio, symbol, graphics, text or a suitable combination of these according to the technical characteristic and practical limitations of the medium.

> Touch the mind create logic and understanding.
> Touch the heart create desire and emotions.
> Touch the mind and the heart and create inspiration and motion.
> - *Albert Einstein, 1928*

Creative Strategy Elements

There are two sets of elements, one which are perceived through the senses, and the other which are comprehended from the stimulus gathered by the senses.

The sensory elements are:

- *Copy* – the verbalised part of the ad, written, spoken, crawling or voice over

- *Illustration and visuals* – the pictures and animations that are worth more than thousand words; and

- *Layout* – the composition of the ad using copy, visuals, sounds, colours, and special effects

The embedded elements are:

- *Ethos* - source of the message - element of persuasiveness due to source effects
- *Pathos* - mood and emotion, and
- *Logos* - logic and rational support arguments

Creative Styles

Like any form of art or thought, the field of advertising has seen some maestros and whizzes, who have left some indelible marks through their signature creative styles. Such styles, like the schools of philosophy or genres of music, have become the hallmark of advertising. Some of the most popular *ragas* of advertising are:

- ❖ **Brand Image** (by David Ogilvy)
- ❖ **Execution** (by William Bernbach)
- ❖ **Unique Selling Proposition** (by Rosser Reeves)
- ❖ **Common Touch** (by Leo Burnett)
- ❖ **Entertainment & Emotion** (by Phil Dussenbery-BBDO)
- ❖ **Irreverence** (by Lee Clow - TBWA)
- ❖ **Small Town Warmth** (by Hal Riney -BBDO)
- ❖ **Empathy** (by Norman B Norman)

Creative Approaches

The meaning embedded in the message could be invoking the rationale or logic, or the emotion or psyche. The former are called the

RATIONAL CREATIVE APPROACHES while the latter are called the **EMOTIONAL CREATIVE APPROACHES.**

The examples of advertisements used as illustrations of the concepts below are subject to the following DISCLAIMERS:
- Not every advertisement fits into this classification.
- One ad may fit into more than one category.
- Not everyone agree with a particular classification- not even with the examples used here.

Rational Creative Approaches take the following three forms:

- *Comparative Advertising*
    - There is evidence that it is a more effective approach
    - Especially when aimed at expert consumers.
    - Or when comparison is made with specific, well-known brand(s)
    - Two sided approach is more effective
    - There is a risk of audience not believing the claim
        - e.g. ...Any 100 cc mobike gives 80 kmpl but... - Kawasaki Bajaj ...

- *Inoculative Advertising*
    - Develops resistance to competitive appeals.
    - Makes brand offering more effective.
    - Trains audience to resist competitive persuasive efforts.
    - Also called the bio-approach.
        - e.g. All others wash, this one cleans - BPL washing machine.

- *Refutational Advertising*
    - Explicit or implicit mention of competitive appeals followed by a refutation of those claims.
    - The approach in itself is more stimulating than the supporting message carried.
    - Refutation ebbs the credibility of the competition.
        - *e.g. Veeba Ketchup*

Emotional Creative Approaches

These approaches make use of devices called the ADVERTISING APPEALS which solicit specific consumer responses and which form the underlying content of the advertisements.

The ways in which the appeals are transformed into advertising and the ways of presenting the content are called the ADVERTISING THEMES/ EXECUTIONS.

The distinctions would be clearer through the examples that follow.

APPEALS
- An appeal is the persuasive part of advertising message
- It is persuasive information (in case information content is present)

THEMES
- A theme is the way you put across your appeal.

An appeal may be transformed or executed in a variety of ways.
- *Example: Palmolive & Godrej Shave-creams used the same appeal but different executions (themes).*

Same Theme or Execution technique may be used with different appeals.

- *Example: Kapil Dev as spokesperson for Action Shoes, Hajmola, Boost, Rapidex English Speaking Course and Pepsi*

Advertising Appeals could be broadly categorised under three groups

Product or Service Related Appeals
- what is there in the product for the audience to take notice of:

Consumer Related Appeals
- What benefit accrues to the consumer in case she considers the advertised product Service.

Non-Consumer, Non-Product/Service Related Appeals
- Relates to non-traditional marketing situations like money from Public, creating a corporate positioning, a PR exercise etc....

Product or Service Related Appeals can take six variants
- Feature Appeals
  - Description of the product and its dominant features, no comparisons or mentioning of price or popularity - e.g. many mobile phone brands like appo,
- Comparative Advantage Appeals
  - explicit reference to competitive products - e.g. PCL pcs
- Favourable Price Appeals
  - Direct offer at a particular or reduced price - e.g. Akai, Sansui etc.

- News Appeals
    - News about product -new/improved/modified e.g. Surf ultra
- Popularity Appeals
    - widely used, popular or number of customers e.g Kelvinator refrigerators
- Generic Appeals
    - Promotion of a product class or category without any brand being singled out e.g. Public Sector Banks (IBA)

Consumer Related Appeals can take four variations

- Consumer Service Appeals
    - what to do with the product/where all to use it e.g. Milkmaid, Triputhy instant foods
- Consumer Saving through Use Appeals
    - Save on experience or consumption, emphasis on saving & NOT on price e.g. Hero Honda - fill it, shut it, forget it
- Consumer Self Enhancement Appeals
    - Enhance or improve quality of user or bring tangible pleasure or satisfaction e.g. Fair & Lovely
- Fear Appeals
    - resolving of a threatening (physical or economic) situation through use (issue of thresholds) e.g. Cease Fire, Insurance
- Subsidized Product Trial Appeals
    - A free sample, price reduction or some other purchase incentive e.g. Airtel.

Non-Product/ Service, Non-Consumer Related Appeals may have two variants

- Corporate Citizenship
    - Good Citizen
    - the other side of the controversy
    - etc.

- Investor Solicitation
    - Well managed
    - Profitable
    - Safe investments or good returns
    - Wide product range, etc.

Advertising Themes have at least twelve known variants

- Factual - Straight forward Execution
    - Hardly a classification, the product is just advertised showing whatever the advertiser likes to say e.g...IFB washing machines.

- Factual - Provocative or Intriguing Statements
    - Facts are stated in a way as to evoke interest, element of curiosity e.g. Rolls Royce - at 60 mph the loudest noise inside came from the clock.

- Product Comparison
    - Comparison with brand, product class, of features or strengths e.g. PCL computers

- Demonstration
    - Of features or strengths e.g. Videocon Washing Machines

- Still Life.
    - Stark representation of the product, no further information on features or benefits given, however some cues for reminder or association may be provided e.g. Smirnoff (liquor), McDowells
- The Metaphor - Imputed Qualities
    - No direct or literal relationship between the product & the association used e.g. Marlboro, Zakir Hussain for Taj tea
- Dramatisation
    - Some sort of drama created around the product-more suited to the audio-visual media e.g. Garden sarees.
- Spokesperson - Just Speaks
    - May be an unknown person or a celebrity- usually mixed with some other theme - e.g... Pepsodent
- Testimony - Speaks with Experience
    - The spokesperson seems to testify out of (personal) experience e.g Vicks Hotsip, Sachin Tendulkar for Action Shoes, Palmolive da jawab nahin
- Borrowed Interest
    - High inherent interest borrowed from elsewhere but no direct relationship e.g. UNICEF cards
- Humour
    - may not be humorous to all, may overwhelm, humour and satire are different, e.g. Cherry Blossom
- Hyperbole - Exaggeration
    - Exaggerate a point about some fact related to the product e.g. Spectrawide.

Brand Communications

Last 100 years have seen the emergence of brands as the most expensive yet intangible assets of business. With technology making the products nearly identical, real product differentials are difficult to sustain. Customers do not have the cognitive strength to resolve and perceive miniscule product differences and value them. Brands are therefore the attribute that consumers use in making buying preferences.

The ability and possibility to use same brands or their variants for multiple product and service offerings by an enterprise makes brand-communications and brand-management as a great new arena for marketing. Significant knowledge checkpoints are listed here:

Brands and their benefits

Temporal Identity and Meaning

- Practicality of Choice (and Performance)
- Permanence and Bonding
- Pleasure of Buying and Consuming
- Ethical and Social Responsibility of Actions

Spatial Identity and Meaning

- Recognition
- Optimisation of Choice
- Guarantee of Quality Perception and Experience
- Personalisation of Choice

Brand Equity

- Added Value empowered to products/services
- Customer-based brand equity
- Brand Equity Models – various approaches

Building Brand Equity

- Brand Elements
- Choice criteria for Elements
- Designing holistic Activities
    - Personalisation
    - Integration
    - Internalisation

Measuring Brand Equity

- Brand Audits
- Brand Tracking
- Brand Valuation
- Brand Asset Valuator
    - Aaker Model
    - Brandz
    - Brand Resonance

Branding Strategy

- To brand or not to brand
- Brand Extensions
- Brand Portfolios
- Managing Brands
    - Reinforcement
    - Revitalisation
    - Crisis

Brand Positioning

- Frame of Reference
- Competitive Parity & Ideal-Point Methods

- Points of Parity
- Points of Differentiation
- Realign Product and Brand Strategy to PLC
- Market Evolution – Emergence, growth, maturity and decline

An Alternate Perspective to Brands

- Branding – a strategic point of view and not a set of activities
- Branding is about creating customer value and not just imagery
- Tool for competitive advantage
- Brands are cultures that circulate in society as stories
- Brand value has four components – Reputation value, Relationship value, Experiential value and Symbolic value

Creativity in Advertising

Creativity as a function of Divergence and Relevance		
	Divergent	*Non-divergent*
Relevant	**Creative**	Relevant but common
Non-relevant	Divergent but irrelevant	**Non-creative**

Smith, R.E. and Yang, X. (2004) "A Theory of Creativity in Advertising", *Marketing Theory*, 4 (1/2): 31-58

- the most fundamental characteristic of ad creativity is divergence (i.e., the ad must contain elements that deviate from the norm and stand out in some way).
- the ad must also be relevant- the ad must be "meaningful, appropriate or valuable to the audience".

- Ad-consumer relevance occurs when the eye-catching elements of the ad are somehow meaningful to the consumer. Brand-consumer relevance occurs when an ad links the brand and the consumer in a meaningful way.

- A third component of creativity in advertising is - the ad must be capable of achieving certain goals and its effects must somehow be quantifiable.

How Brand Awareness helps? (Courtesy: Aaker)

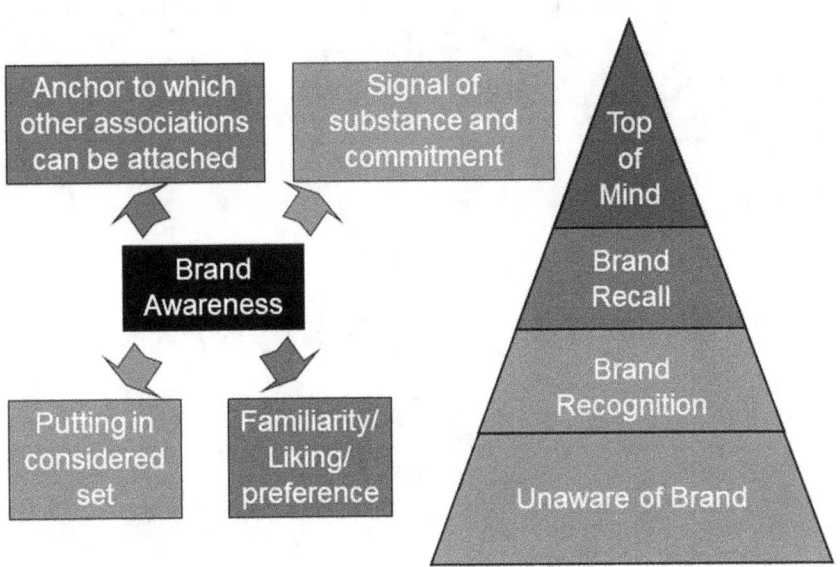

Achieving Brand Awareness

Achieving awareness (at any level) involves two tasks: establishing a brand name identity and linking it to the product class.
- Be different and memorable
- Use a slogan or jingle
- Event Sponsorship
- The recall bonus

Value of Brand Associations (courtesy: Aaker)

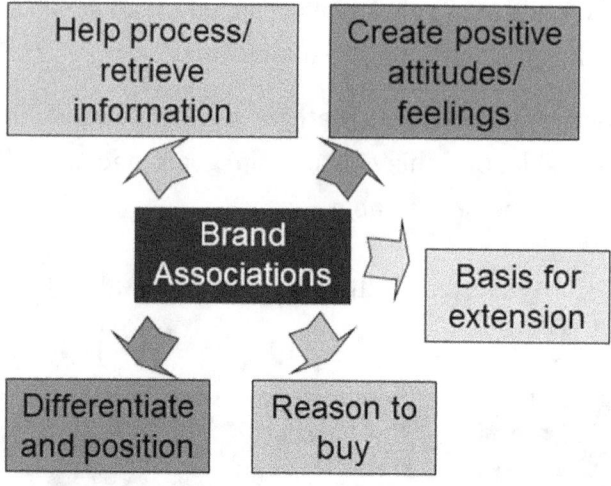

Types of Brand Association (Courtesy: Keller)

Communications for Brands

- Branding is to enhance the perceived value of the product.
- Branding consists of four different types of value creation:
    - Build quality reputation
    - Build perceptions that company is a good relationship partner
    - Frame how consumers perceive product experiences
    - Imbue the brand, as a symbol, with values and identities

Six Creative Decision Filters

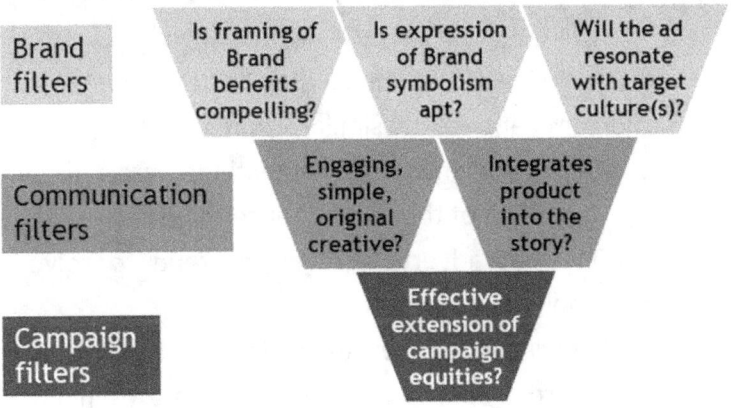

- Ads work (or not) within thematic structures we call campaigns.
- A campaign can be like a serial on television, with the same characters meeting each week to act out similar plots. Alternatively, the same director can hold a campaign together as a stylistic unity — like a series of films—where the communication elements bind the ads together.

- Ads are not isolated communication efforts, as they are often treated, but rather components of this larger entity.
- A good ad builds on the previous ads in the campaign, advancing strategic goals to extend the campaign.

Media Strategy

- Concerns with how advertising messages will be delivered to the audience
- Involves –
    - Identification of the characteristics of audience who would receive the advertising messages
    - Defining of media objectives that must be met in the delivery of the advertising messages
- There is no single best media strategy that applies to every situation or in apparently similar situations
    - Any two marketing situations are rarely alike regardless of their appearance to be
    - Different advertisers/agencies tend to solve media problems in different ways
    - Knowledge about advertising media and the exact nature of contribution that media makes in advertising process is imperfect
    - Different advertisers in the same industry spend their advertising budgets differently
    - Basic patterns of media expenditures change over time
    - New media class and media vehicles are evolving

"You aren't advertising to a standing army; you are advertising to a moving parade...they (consumers) enter the market and they depart from it. An advertisement is like a radar sweep, constantly hunting new prospects as they come into the market..." - David Ogilvy

Issues in Advertising Media Strategy

- The kind of consumers that advertiser wishes to reach –
    - Understanding those to be reached
    - MEDIA that would REACH the target audience exclusively or to a greater extent than non-target audience
    - Trying to match audience-information with media-audience information
    - Trying to limit the number of dimensions by which ad-audience are described
- The kind of message dispersion required –
    - Reach smaller audience more times or large audience less times
    - Delivery of message AT LEAST ONCE to as many prospects as possible
    - A good general rule is to have a plan that concentrates message delivery at the middle of the frequency range rather than at the extremes
- The kind of seasonal and/or regional concentration required for advertising –
    - Seasonal/regional scatter of advertising
    - Lead and lag between effort and required response
    - Frequency of response and weight of response
- Qualities that should be inherent in the media –
    - Qualitative media effects – what the medium does to enhance or depreciate the message
    - This may occur due to editorial climate, attitude of audience towards the editorial content or the particular kind of audience being attracted towards it due to its own features

- The extent of necessity to have total isolation from competing messages
- The clutter of advertising
- Media effects on message may not affect the quality of audience response required but the quality and efficiency of message delivery is affected
- Implications of the advertising message content –
  - Whole advertising effort is related to
    - Message content that would cause desired consumer response
    - Characteristics of target audience
  - First has creative strategy implications and the second has media strategy implications
  - So, high interface between creative strategy and media strategy – creative strategy may cause limitations for media choice

Understanding Message Dispersion

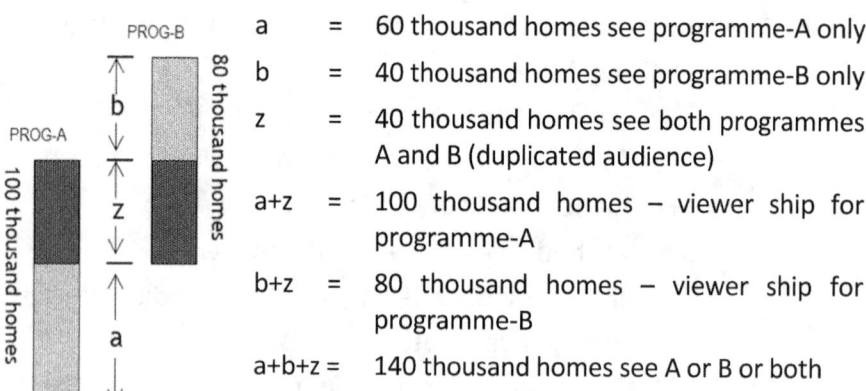

a = 60 thousand homes see programme-A only
b = 40 thousand homes see programme-B only
z = 40 thousand homes see both programmes A and B (duplicated audience)
a+z = 100 thousand homes – viewer ship for programme-A
b+z = 80 thousand homes – viewer ship for programme-B
a+b+z = 140 thousand homes see A or B or both

Gross Homes Reached = viewer ship of A + viewer ship of B = 180 thousand homes
Net coverage/ REACH /accumulated audience = 140 thousand homes
FREQUENCY = GROSS REACHED/REACH = 180 thousand/140 thousand = 1.3

Qualitative Factors in Media Decisions
- Media Class decisions –
    - Print Media
    - Audio-visual Media
    - Direct Advertising
    - Out of Home Media
    - Internet/Interactive Media
    - Fit between Media and Creative
        - TV good for emotional, image or demonstrations but poor for highly factual ads
        - Print- offers colour values – can take complex messages
        - Bill boards – only recognition possible
        - Radio- for involvement (but suffers from Clutter)
    - Production Logistics
    - Competitive Setting
- Media Vehicle decisions –
    - Print – which Newspapers or Magazines, etc.
    - Differential impact due to
        - Editorial environment
        - Physical production values
        - Audience involvement
    - Vehicle attributes
        - Unbiased ness
        - Expertness
        - Prestige
        - Mood created
        - Audience involvement
    - Qualitative Publication Index

- - Competitive Advertising Volume (e.g. Total number of pages)
    - Editorial Content (percentage of space devoted to subjects pertaining to product)
    - Editorial Quality (ratio of edit/ad pages)
    - Qualitative Factors in Media Decisions
- Media Option decisions –
  - What unit of advertising to be employed?
  - size, length, colour, location
- Scheduling and timing decisions –
  - Flighting (bursts of advertising alternated with total blackout)
  - Continuous/Even (advertising spread evenly through the campaign time period)
  - Pulsing (a continuous base augmented by intermittent burst of heavy advertising)

Media Classes

Print Media

- Print advertising includes printed advertisements in newspapers, magazines, brochures, posters, and outdoor boards
- Print provides more detailed information, rich imagery, and a longer message life

Print Media: Newspapers

- Used by advertisers trying to reach a local market
- Primary function is to carry news

- Market selectivity allows newspapers to target specific consumer groups
- Considerations -
    - Frequency of publication
    - Format and size
    - Circulation
- Types of Advertising
    - Classified
    - Display
    - Supplements
- Newspaper Readership
    - Tends to be highest among older people and people with a higher educational level
- Advantages
    - Range of market coverage
    - Comparison shopping
    - Positive consumer attitudes
    - Flexibility
    - Interaction of national and local ads
- Disadvantages
    - Short life span
    - Clutter
    - Limited coverage of certain groups
    - Poor reproduction
- Use Newspapers If...
    - You are a local business
    - Desire extensive market coverage
    - Product is consumed in a predictable manner
    - No need to demonstrate the product
    - Moderate to large budget

Print Media: Magazines

- Most magazines today are special interest publications aimed at narrower target markets
- Specialty magazines seem to have an edge over more general publications in terms of maintaining growth
- Upscale magazines provide an ideal place for the image advertising of luxury products
- Distribution and Circulation
    - Traditional delivery
    - Through newsstand purchases or home delivery
    - Non-traditional delivery (controlled circulation)
    - Hanging bagged copies on doorknobs
    - Inserting magazines in newspapers
    - Delivering through professionals
    - Direct delivery
- Types of Magazines
    - Audience focus
        - Consumer magazines
        - Business magazines
        - Industry/ Farm magazines
    - Other classifications
        - Geography
        - Demographics
        - Editorial content
        - Physical characteristics
        - Ownership

- Advertising Formats
    - Double-page spread
    - Gutter
    - Bleed page
    - Gatefold
    - Photo essay ad
- Technology has enabled magazines to distinguish themselves from one another
- Advantages of Magazine Advertising
    - Target audience
    - Audience receptivity
    - Long life span
    - Format
    - Visual quality
    - Sales promotions
- Disadvantages of Magazine Advertising
    - Limited flexibility
    - Lack of immediacy
    - High cost
    - Distribution
- Use Magazines If...
    - Well-defined target audience
    - Want to reinforce or remind audience
    - Product must be shown accurately and beautifully
    - Need to relate moderate to extensive information
    - Moderate to large budget

Out-of-Home Media

- Billboards and posters in public locations
- On-Premise Signs
- Retail signs that identify stores

- Posters
- Used on the sides of buildings and vehicles, as well as on bulletin boards
- Kiosks
- Designed for public posting of notices and advertising posters
- Transit advertising
- Includes posters in bus, train, airport, and subway stations
- Size and format
    - Printed posters
    - Painted bulletin
- Buying Out-of-Home Media
    - Showings
    - Traffic count Advantages
- Advantages of Out-of-Home Media
    - High impact medium
    - Larger-than-life visuals
    - Hard to ignore structure
    - Least expensive
- Disadvantages of Out-of-Home Media
    - Message could fail to be seen or have impact
    - Passive medium
    - Extensive regulation
- Use Out-of-Home If...
    - Local business that wants to sell locally
    - Regional or national business that wants to remind or reinforce
    - Product requires little information and little demonstration
    - Small to moderate budget

Broadcast Media

- Transmit sounds or images electronically
- Include radio and television
- Broadcast engages more senses than reading and adds audio as well as motion for television

Broadcast Media: Radio

- Structure of the Industry
    - AM/FM
    - Public radio
    - Cable radio
    - Satellite radio
    - LPFM
    - Web radio
- Radio Advertising
    - Relies on the listener's mind to fill in the visual element
    - Delivers a high level of frequency
    - Radio commercials lead themselves to repetition
    - Offers advertisers a variety of high-quality, specialized, and usually original programs
    - Advertisers value syndicated programming because of the high level of audience loyalty
- The Radio Audience
    - Station fans
        - Largest segment of radio listeners
        - A clear preference for one or two stations
    - Radio fans
        - May listen to four or five stations per week
        - Show no preference for one particular station

- - Music fans
    - People who listen exclusively for the music being played
  - News fans
    - Choose stations based on a need for news and information
    - Have 1-2 favourite stations
- Advantages of Radio
  - Target audience
  - Affordability
  - Frequency
  - Flexibility
  - Mental imagery
  - High level of acceptance
- Disadvantages of Radio
  - Listener inattentiveness
  - Lack of visuals
  - Clutter
  - Scheduling and buying difficulties
  - Lack of control

Broadcast Media: Television
- Television advertising is embedded in television programming
- Most of the attention in media buying, and in measuring effectiveness, focuses on the performance of various shows and how they engage their audiences
  - Mobile Video Reorders
  - TV on mobile phones
  - High-definition TV
  - Interactive television

- Network television
    - When two or more stations are able to broadcast the same program that originates from a single source
    - Networks originate programs and provide them to local affiliates
- Cable and subscription
    - Provide highly targeted special-interest programming options
    - Cable is most familiar example of subscription television
- Local television
    - Carry network programming and their own programs
- Affiliated with a network
- Public television
    - Many consider public television to be commercial-free
    - Stations can air program sponsorship ads
- Sponsorships
    - Advertiser assumes total financial responsibility for producing the program and providing the commercials
    - Advertiser can control the content and quality of the program and the placement and length of commercials
- Participations
    - Where advertisers pay for 10, 15, 20, 30, or 60 seconds of commercial time during a program
    - Provides more flexibility in market coverage, target audiences, scheduling, and budgeting
- Spot announcements
    - Commercials that appear in the breaks between programs
    - Local affiliates sell these to advertisers who want to show their ads locally

- Advantages
    - Pervasiveness
    - Cost efficiency
    - Impact
- Disadvantages
    - Production costs
    - Clutter
    - Wasted reach
    - Inflexibility
    - Intrusiveness

Film and Video

- Trailers
    - Videocassette and DVD distributors also placing ads before movies
    - Promotional video networks in stores, offices, truck stops, etc.
    - Advantages of using Trailers
        - Play to a captive audience
        - Attention level is higher than for almost any other form of commercials
    - Disadvantages of using Trailers
        - Captive audience resents intrusion of ads
- Product Placement
    - When a company pays to have verbal or visual brand exposure in a movie or TV program
    - Advantages of Product Placement
        - Demonstrates product usage in a natural setting by celebrities
        - Catches audience when resistance to ads is low

- Disadvantages of Product Placement
    - May not be noticed
    - Not a match between product/ movie/ audience

Using Broadcast Advertising

- *Use Radio If...*
    - Local business
    - Highly targeted audience
    - Small budget
    - Timing consideration
    - Align interests with program
    - Personal message with human voice
    - Works in musical form or strong in mental imagery
    - Need reminder message
- *Use Television If...*
    - Want wider mass audience
    - Align interests with program
    - Good budget
    - Product needs both sight and sound
    - Prove something to audience
    - Halo effect
    - Create or reinforce brand image and personality
- *Use Movie Ads If...*
    - National brand
    - Have budget to do high-quality commercials
    - Want to associate brand with movie stars
    - Movie audience matches brand's target audience
    - Substantial visual impact and quality production

- *Use Placement If...*
    - Want to associate brand with stars and story
    - Viewing audience matches brand's target audience
    - Natural fit between product and storyline
    - Opportunity for brand as star
    - Appeals to stakeholders
    - Supporting ad campaign

Interactive Media

- Communication systems that permit two-way communication
- Believed to be the most persuasive type of communication available to marketers
- Not limited to the Internet – also includes telephone and e-mail

- *Internet*
    - Web sites
    - Advertising resources
    - Search engines
    - Search marketing
    - B2B ad networks
    - Chat rooms
    - Blogs
    - The Internet Audience
        - The Internet is the leading tool for information searching by all ages
        - Teens spend more time online than any other age group
    - Measuring Audiences
        - Hits

- The number of times a particular site is visited
- Click-through
- The number of people who click on a banner ad
- Internet Advertising: Primary Purposes
  - Provide a brand reminder message
  - Deliver informational or persuasive message
  - Drive traffic
- Types of Internet Ads
  - Banner ads
  - Skyscrapers
  - Pop-ups/Pop-behinds
  - Minisites
  - Superstitials
  - Rich media
  - Streaming video
- E-Mail Advertising
  - Spam
  - Unsolicited messages sent to e-mail in-boxes
  - Opt-in
  - Bulk e-mailers have to get permission to send
  - Opt-out
  - E-mailers have to have an option to say no to further e-mails
- Viral Marketing
  - Uses e-mail to circulate a message among family and friends
- Internet Advertising: Advantages
  - Relatively inexpensive
  - Can also deliver business
  - Advertisers can customize and personalize messages

- Can provide sales leads or actual sales
- Internet Advertising: Disadvantages
  - Inability of experts to consistently produce effective ads and to measure their effectiveness
  - Clutter may even be worse than in other media

Alternative and New Media

- *Advertainment*
  - When companies integrate brands into the content of shows
  - Also called branded entertainment
  - Situational ads
  - Harder for the viewer to dismiss as ads
  - Product is a character in the program
- *New Internet Practices*
  - Brand experiences on the Web
  - Companies making their Web sites more engaging and entertaining
  - Webisodes
  - Recurring episodes in a developing story
  - Blends advertising and entertainment to attract audiences
- *Video Games*
  - Opportunities to create online games as well as place products within video games
  - Planners and buyers are asking for standardized independent data that prove effectiveness
- *Guerrilla Marketing*
  - Unconventional marketing communication activities
  - Intended to get a buzz on a limited budget

- *Wireless Communication*
    - Links the common phone to a computer
    - The most important change in communication systems in the new millennium
- *Non-electronic New Media*
    - Ads appearing in unexpected new places

Media Planning

Thomas Smith wrote a guide called *Successful Advertising* in 1885. We can see its relevance to this day.

- The first time a man looks at an advertisement, he does not see it.
- The second time, he does not notice it.
- The third time, he is conscious of its existence.
- The fourth time, he faintly remembers having seen it before.
- The fifth time, he reads it.
- The sixth time, he turns up his nose at it.
- The seventh time, he reads it through and says, "Oh brother!"
- The eighth time, he says, "Here's that confounded thing again!"
- The ninth time, he wonders if it amounts to anything.
- The tenth time, he asks his neighbour if he has tried it.
- The eleventh time, he wonders how the advertiser makes it pay.
- The twelfth time, he thinks it must be a good thing.
- The thirteenth time, he thinks perhaps it might be worth something.
- The fourteenth time, he remembers wanting such a thing a long time.
- The fifteenth time, he is tantalized because he cannot afford to buy it.
- The sixteenth time, he thinks he will buy it someday.
- The seventeenth time, he makes a memorandum to buy it.
- The eighteenth time, he swears at his poverty.
- The nineteenth time, he counts his money carefully.
- The twentieth time he sees the ad, he buys what it is offering.

Media Selection and Scheduling

- This is the issue of finding the best way to deliver the "desired number of exposures" to the target audience and to schedule the delivery of those exposures over the planning period.
- Desired number of exposures
    - Advertising aims at some response like Trial rate, Purchase, etc.
    - Response is a function of exposures but response increases at a diminishing rate with increasing exposure.

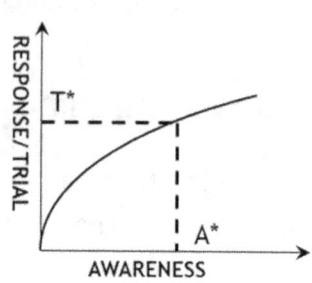

    - Say, for example – if advertiser wants to achieve a product trial-rate T*, it must achieve a Brand Awareness rate of A*, and the task is to find out how many exposures, E* are needed to produce this awareness.
    - The effect of exposures on audience awareness depends on the REACH, FREQUENCY and IMPACT of exposures.

Reach, Frequency and Impact

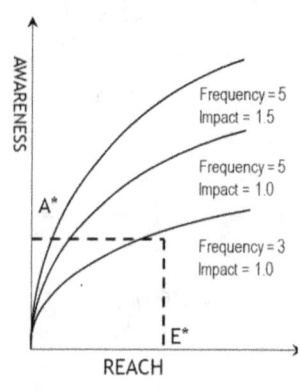

Reach (R) - The number of different persons or households exposed to a particular media schedule at least once during a specified time period.

Frequency (F) - The number of times within the specified time period that an average person or household is exposed to the message.

Impact (I) – The qualitative value of an exposure through a given medium (A food product ad may have higher impact in 'Femina' than in 'Computers Today'

Empirical Findings about Frequency

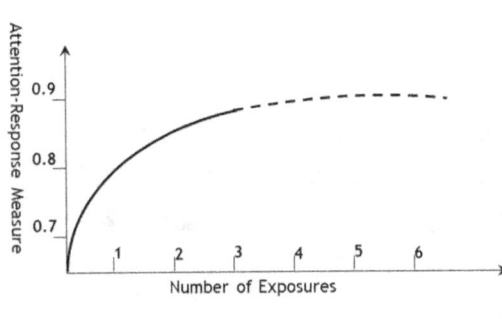

- Optimal exposure frequency appears to be at least three exposures within a purchase cycle
- Beyond 3 (three) exposures, effectiveness increases but at a decreasing rate.

- Frequency by itself does not cause wear-out, although it can advance the decline of an effective campaign
- Response to advertising appears smaller for the brand with dominant market share

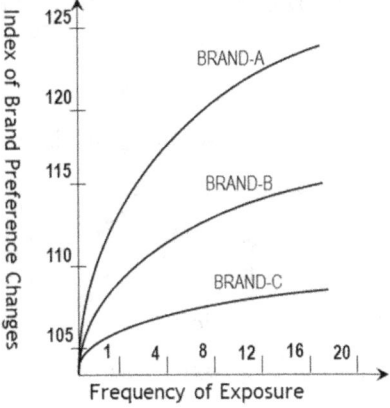

Reach, Frequency and Exposure

- Total number of Exposures (E) = R x F
- This is also called the Gross Rating Points (GRP)
- If a media schedule reaches 60% of the homes with an average exposure Frequency of 3, the Media Schedule has a GRP = 180 (E = R x F)

- If another schedule has a GRP of 240, we can say that it has more weight.
- But this weight cannot be broken down into Reach (R) and Frequency (F)
- Weighted number of exposures (WE) is Total Exposure times the Average Impact

$$WE = I \times E$$
$$= R \times F \times I$$

- The Media Planning Problem can thus be defined as –
With a given budget, what is the Most Cost Effective combination of Reach, Frequency and Impact to buy?

Developing a Media Plan

- Medium is the carrier of the message and not the instrument that accomplishes the final advertising effect
- Media facilitates message delivery because of its reach to more receptive audience
- Each media has its own appeal
- The belief that media audience is also the message audience
- Media exposure intensity is not the same across the population
- Intra-media variations and inter-media variations exist

Decisions Areas in Media Plan

- Multiple media use
- Ad budgets influence media choice
- How many media classes, media types, media options and how much of each
- Media Efficiency – $$\text{Cost per thousand (CPM)} = \frac{\text{Cost of media Unit or Units}}{\text{Media Audience or Circulation}}$$

Media Planning Considerations - Geographic coverage

- Brand and Category Analysis
    - Category Development Index

$$CDI = \frac{\text{Percentage of product category total sales in market}}{\text{Percentage of total Indian population in market}} \times 100$$

    - Brand Development Index

$$BDI = \frac{\text{Percentage of brand sales in market to total Indian sales}}{\text{Percentage of total Indian population in market}} \times 100$$

Media Planning Considerations - Media mix - Target market coverage

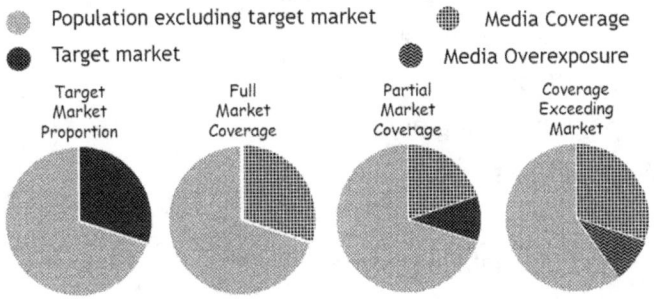

Media Planning Considerations - Reach versus frequency

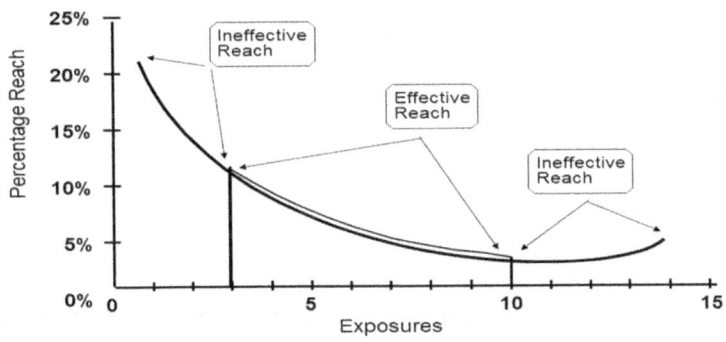

Media Planning Considerations - frequency

- Marketing Factors
    - Brand history
    - Brand share
    - Brand loyalty
    - Purchase cycles
    - Usage cycle
    - Competitive share of voice
    - Target group
- Creative Factors
    - Message complexity
    - Message uniqueness
    - New vs. continuing campaigns
    - Image versus product sell
    - Message variation
    - Wear out
    - Advertising units
- Media Factors
    - Clutter
    - Editorial environment
    - Attentiveness
    - Scheduling
    - Number of media used
    - Repeat Exposures

Modelling Approaches to Media Planning

- There are generally three components in models for media decisions –
    - The objective function, which assigns a value (profit/ effective exposures, etc.) to an insertion schedule

- o The solution strategy – Non-optimisation Approach (Heuristics, Bayesian, step-wise or marginal analysis), Optimisation Approach (Mathematical programming – linear, non-linear, goal) or Simulation Approach (Dynamo and Planex)
  - o The constraints (budgets, others)
- There are generally five principal components of the objective function –
  - o The vehicle exposure measure – used to measure the net reach, schedule exposure, or GRPs
  - o Repetition effect – what is the relative impact of successive exposures on the same person? (research indicates the function is S-shaped)
  - o Forgetting effect – what forgetting occurs between exposures and what is the nature of the decay?
  - o Media-option source effect – what is the relative impact exposure from a given source?
  - o Segmentation effect – who is exposed and what is the fraction of the audience that represents target segments?

Bayesian Approach to Media Planning & Modelling

$P(A \cup B) = P(A) + P(B) - P(A \cap B)$

$P(B/A) = \dfrac{P(A \cap B)}{P(A)} \quad P(A/B) = \dfrac{P(A \cap B)}{P(B)}$

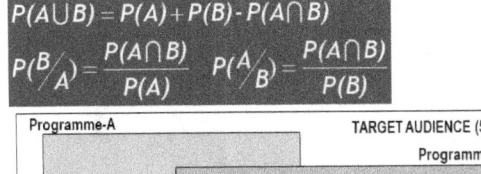

- Duplicated Audience = 15%
- Unduplicated audience = 55%
- Frequency Distribution
  - Exposure   Audience
  - 0   225,000
  - 1   200,000
  - 2   75,000

$P(A) = 0.30 \quad P(B) = 0.40 \quad P(A \cap B) = 0.15$

$P(B/A) = \dfrac{0.15}{0.30} = 0.50 \quad P(A/B) = \dfrac{0.15}{0.40} = 0.375$

Media Planning Models

- *Optimisation Approach – Linear/Non-linear, Integer, Goal, Dynamic*
    - Maximise REACH: : Subject to
        - Cost constraints
        - Vehicle constraints
        - Frequency Constraints

        Or
    - Maximise FREQUENCY: : Subject to
        - Cost constraints
        - Vehicle constraints
        - Reach Constraints
    - Minimise COSTS: : Subject to
        - Reach constraints
        - Vehicle constraints
        - Frequency Constraints

        Or

- *Simulation Approach*
    - Work on real exposure data
    - Data obtained from a sample of audience
    - SIMULATE for determining what the reach and frequency would be
    - Modify by objectives

- *Heuristics Approach (e.g. MEDIAC)*
    - Develop a superior (not necessarily optimal) model
    - Add vehicles to the schedule based on Marginal contribution (CPM, Frequency, etc.)

Scheduling and Timing Decisions

u = Ad Spends
t = Time
ū = Peak ad spend beyond which ad effectiveness is subject to diminishing returns
T = Campaign Plan time Period
α = Minimum time period for advertising effects to trigger in

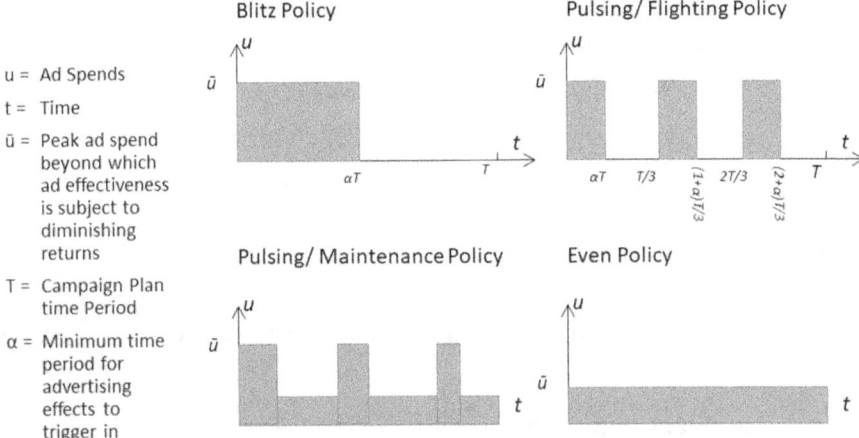

Direct Response Communications – Database Marketing

- Occurs when a seller and customers deal with each other directly
- Four tools of direct marketing
    o Catalogue
    o Direct mail
    o Telemarketing
    o Direct response advertising

Direct Marketing

- *Advantages of Direct Marketing*
    o Collection of relevant customer information
    o Purchase not restricted to a location
    o The marketer controls product until delivery
    o Easier to evaluate

- o Flexibility in form and timing
- *Disadvantages of Direct Marketing*
  - o Consumers are still reluctant to purchase a product they have not seen or touched
  - o Annoyances associated with direct marketing
  - o Unable to reach everyone in the marketplace

Direct-Response Advertising

- Combines the characteristics of advertising with a contact element
- The direct-marketing process
  - o Objectives and strategies
  - o The offer
  - o Message and media strategy
  - o The response/order
  - o Fulfilment and customer maintenance
  - o Evaluation

Database Marketing

- A practice that uses databases to predict trends and monitor consumers
- Four primary objectives
  - o Record names of customers
  - o Store and measure results of advertising
  - o Store and measure purchasing performance
  - o Vehicle for continuing direct communication
- The Database Marketing Process
  - o Collection point
  - o Data entry
  - o Data assessment

- o Data clustering
- o Data application
- o Data sharing
- o Data refinement

Key Players in Direct Marketing

- Advertisers
    - o Companies whose primary business is selling products and services by mail or telephone
    - o Retail stores who use direct marketing as a supplement to other forms of marketing communication
- Agencies
    - o Advertising agencies
    - o Independent agencies
    - o Service firms
    - o Fulfilment houses
- Media Companies
- The media that deliver messages by phone, mail, or the Web
- Customers
- Recipients of the information and sometimes the initiator of the contact
- Push-button shopper
- Mouse-clicking shopper

The Tools of Direct Marketing

- Direct Mail
    - o A print advertising message for a product or service that is delivered by mail
- Catalogues

- A multi-page direct-mail publication that shows a variety of merchandise
- Growth in this field is in the area of specialty catalogues
- Video catalogues provide more information about products
- Telemarketing
  - Types of telemarketing
  - Criticisms of telemarketing
  - Telemarketing messaging design
- Direct-Response Advertising
  - All direct-response advertising moves the consumer to action
  - Well-targeted
  - Reaches prime audience
- The Internet and Direct Response
  - Same components as direct mail and telemarketing
  - Greater sampling opportunities
  - New ways to gather information

Sales Promotions

- A marketing discipline that utilizes a variety of incentive techniques to structure sales-related programs that generate a specific, measurable action or response
- Growth in Sales Promotion has often been triggered by Pressure for short-term profits
- Managerial Issues in a Move to Sales Promotion
  - Need for accountability
  - Easy to evaluate
  - Consumer behaviour
  - Pricing

- Market share
- Parity products
- Power of the retailer

Consumer Promotions

- Price deals: Temporary price reduction or sale price
    - Rupees-off
    - Price-pack deals
    - Bonus packs
    - Banded packs
- Coupons: Provide a discount on the price of the product
    - Retailer
    - Manufacturer
- Refunds and rebates: Marketer's offer to return a certain amount of money to the consumer
- Sampling: Allowing the consumer to try the product or service
- Contests and sweepstakes
    - Create excitement by promising something for nothing
    - Contests based on skill or ability
    - Sweepstakes based on luck (illegal in India)
- Premiums
- Tangible reward for a particular act
- Work by adding value to the product
    - Store premiums
    - In-pack premiums
    - On-pack premiums
    - Container premiums
- Specialties
    - Presents the brand's name on something that is given away as a reminder

Trade Promotions

- Point-of-purchase display
    - Manufacturer-designed display distributed to retailers
    - Retailers use the displays to call their customer's attention to product promotions
- Retailer kits
    - Materials that support retailer's selling efforts or help representatives make sales calls on prospective retailing customers
- Trade incentives and deals
    - When a manufacturer rewards a seller financially for purchase or support
- Buying allowances
- Advertising allowances
- Contests
    - Advertisers can develop contests and sweepstakes to motivate resellers
    - Contests far more common
- Trade shows and exhibits
    - When companies in the same industry gather to present and sell their merchandise and to demonstrate products

Public Relations

- Used to generate goodwill for an organization
- Helps an organization and its publics relate to each other
- Media use
    - Public relations people seek to persuade media gatekeepers to carry stories about their companies

- o This aspect of PR is called publicity
- Control
  - o In the case of news stories, public relations people are at the mercy of the media gatekeeper
  - o Advertising runs exactly as the client who paid for it has approved
- Credibility
  - o The public tends to trust the media more than they do advertisers
  - o Implied third-party endorsement

Types of Public Relations Programmes

- Media relations
  - o Focuses on developing media contacts
  - o Knowing who in the media might be interested in the organization's story
- Employee relations
  - o Programs that communicate information to employees
  - o Internal marketing
  - o Communication efforts aimed at informing employees about marketing programs
- Financial relations
  - o Efforts aimed at the financial community
- Public affairs
  - o Corporate communication programs with government and with the public on issues related to government and regulation
    - Lobbying
    - Issue management
- Fund-raising
  - o The practice of raising money by collecting donations

- Cause marketing
  - When companies associate themselves with a cause, providing assistance and financial support

Retail Advertising

- Retail marketing is about selling and shopping
- Occurs on local, national, and international levels
- Accounts for nearly half of all the money spent on advertising

Retail Advertising Objectives

- Build store traffic
- Build store brand awareness
- Sell a variety of products and brands
- Deliver sales promotion messages
- Create and communicate store image
- Establish store brand that resonates with audience
- Create customer desire to shop

Retail Advertising Strategies

- Cooperative advertising
  - When the national brand reimburses the retailer for part or all of the advertising expenses
  - Ad allowances
- Institutional and product retail advertising
  - Institutional retail advertising sells the retail store as a brand
  - Product retail advertising presents specific merchandise for sale at a certain price

The Media of Retail Advertising

- Local retailers prefer reach over frequency
- Newspapers and direct mail largest local retail advertising media

B2B Advertising

- Industrial advertising
    - Directed at original equipment manufacturers
- Government advertising
    - Largest purchaser of industrial goods
    - Such goods may be advertised in government-targeted publications
- Trade/channel advertising
    - Used to persuade distribution channel members to stock the products of the manufacturer
- Professional advertising
    - Directed at mostly white-collar workers or advertising/marketing specialists
- Agricultural advertising
    - Promotes a variety of products and services
        - Animal health products
        - Seeds & Fertilisers, pesticides
        - Machinery and farm-equipment

Non-profit or Social Marketing

- *Cause/Mission Marketing*
    - Adopting a good cause and sponsoring community and fund-raising efforts
    - Links a company's mission and core values to a cause

- *Non-profit Marketing*
    - Fundraising
    - Public communication campaigns

"I have learned that any fool can write a bad ad, but that it takes a real genius to keep his hands off a good one." – Leo Burnett

A successful mind is the one that is always hungry for learning. While each human being is born with a passion to learn, somewhere, by the passage of time, we lose excitement and passion for learning. The pressure to excel in any arena, be it advertising too, robs the people of the willingness to learn. People those who stick to the basics and stick to what they know from previous endeavours can never excel in advertising. They fail to take risks and advertising and marketing is all about risk. These kinds of people always try to fix the creativity to their mental evolvement. For excelling in the arena of advertising, one must be motivated to take risks, learn, unlearn and then to relearn. This principle not only helps in the industry, but also helps in one's personal growth.

"Creativity may well be the last legal unfair competitive advantage we can take to run over the competition." – Dave Trott

Reference

Aaker, David A., Rajeev Batra & John G. Myers (1992) *Advertising Management*, New Delhi: Prentice Hall of India, 4th ed. pp.537-42, 564

Achenbaum, Alvin A. (1972) "Advertising Doesn't Manipulate Consumers" *Journal of Advertising Research*, 12:12

Ackoff, Russell L. and James R. Emshoff (1975) "Advertising Research at Anheuser Busch Inc. (1963-68)", *Sloan Management Review*, 16:3, pp.1-15

Albion, Mark S. and Paul W. Farris (1979) "Appraising Research On Advertising's Economic Impacts" Cambridge, Mass: *Marketing Science Institute Report* #79-115 pp.29

Andrew Hacker (2010). *"Two Nations: Black and White, Separate, Hostile, Unequal"*, p.37, Simon and Schuster

Andrew S. C. Ehenberg (1974). "Repetitive Advertising and The Consumer" *Journal of Advertising Research*, 14:25, April.

Arndt, Johan (1976) "What is Wrong With Advertising Research" *Journal of Advertising Research*, Vol. 16, no. 3, June pp.9-18

Boddewyn, J. J. (1980). "Decency and Sexism in Advertising: Findings of an I. A. A. A. sponsored 37 Nation Survey of Their Regulation and Self Regulation", *Solus*, Vol. 15, No 6.

Bogart, Leo (1978). "Is All This Advertising Necessary?" *Journal of Advertising Research*, 18:24 October.

Borden, Neil H. (1942) *The Economic Effects of Advertising*, Richard D Irwin Inc., pp. 988. Chap. 2

Britt, Steuart Henderson and Boyd, Harper W. (1978) *Marketing Management and Administrative Action*, McGraw-Hill Inc., US; 4th Revised edition

Brown, Robert George (1974) "Sales Response to Promotion and Advertising", *Journal of Advertising Research*, vol. 14, No. 4, August. pp 33-39.

Calkins, Earnest Elmo (1924) *"Louder, Please, The Autobiography of a Deaf Man*, Boston: The Atlantic Monthly Press, p. 4.

Calkins, Earnest Elmo and Ralph Holden (1905). *Modern Advertising*, New York: D. Appleton and Co., p. 63

Cantor, Nancy Walter Mischel (1977) "Traits as Prototypes: Effects on Recognition Memory," *Journal of Personality and Social Psychology*, vol. 33 January, pp. 38-48.

Carnegie Mellon University Marketing Seminar (1978). "Attitude Change or Attitude Formation? An Unanswered Question," *Journal of Consumer Research*, vol. 4, March, pp. 271-6.

Charles Ramond (1976). *Advertising Research: The State of the Art*, New York: Association of National Advertisers, Inc., p. 96.

Corkindale, David R. and Sherril H. Kennedy (1975). *Measuring the Effect of Advertising: A Comprehensive Approach*, DC Health Ltd., Saxen House, Hants, p. 10.

Cox, Donald F. (1969) "The Audience Ad Communicators," in *Measuring Advertising Effectiveness*, John Wheatley, editor, Homewood, Illinois: Richard D. Irwin, Inc., p. 211.

Dalbey, Homer M., Irwin Gross and Yoram Wind (1968). *Advertising Measurement and Decision Making* Boston: Allyn & Becon, Inc.

Darrell, B. Lucas, (1974) "Review of Frontiers of Advertising Theory & Research", *Journal of Marketing Research*, 11:469, November.

Dickson, Peter R, and Paul W. Miniard (1978). "A Further Examination of Two Laboratory Tests of the Extended Fishbein Attitude Model," *Journal of Consumer Research*, vol. 4 March, pp. 261-6.

Dixit Avinash and Victor Norman (1978), "Advertising and Welfare" *The Bell Journal of Economics*, Vol. 9, No. 1 (spring, 1978), pp. 1-17 Published By: RAND Corporation

Dunn Watson S. (1969). *Advertising: it's Role in Modern Marketing*, 2 ed., Holt, Rhinehart and Winston Inc., p. 92

Evans, W.A. (1974). *Advertising Today and Tomorrow*, London: George Allen & Urwin Ltd.

Faison, Edmond W. J. (1980). *Advertising: A Behaviour Approach for Managers*, New York: John Wiley & Sons, 1980. pp 783, Chapter 23.

Festinger, Leon (1957). *A Theory of Cognitive Dissonance* Stanford: Stanford University Press, pp. 11

Fishbein, Martin (1963). "An Investigation of the Relationships between Beliefs about an Object and the Attitude toward the Object," *Human Relations*, vol. 16, pp. 233-40

Fishbein, Martin (1967). "A Consideration of Beliefs and Their Role in Attitude Measurement," in *Readings in Attitude Theory and Measurement*, Martin Fishbein, ed., New York: John Wiley & Sons, Inc., pp. 257-66.

Fishbein, Martin and Icek Ajzen (1975). *Belief, Attitude, Intention and Behavior: An Introduction to Theory and Research*, Reading, Massachusetts: Addison-Wesley

Foster, G. Allen (1967). *Advertising: Ancient Market Place to Television*, New York: Criterion Books

Fraser, M. (1994). "Quality in Higher Education: an International Perspective" in *What is Quality in Higher Education?* Green, D., ed. Buckingham: Open University press and Society for Research into Higher Education. pp. 101–111

French, George and Harry Tipper (1923). *Advertising Campaigns*, New York: D Van Nostrand Co. Inc., p. 407

Greer, Carl Richard (1940), *Advertising and its Mechanical Production*, New York: Tudor Publishing Co. p. 16

Greyser, Stephen G. (1972). "Advertising Attacks and Counters", *Harvard Business Review*; Vol. 50, No 2, March- April, p. 28

Gupta, Mukul P (1999). Advertising@Improbability.Hope in *Proceedings of 26th National Management Convention* New Delhi: All India Management Association

Gupta, Mukul P (1999). *Collateral Perusal of Advertising Effects*, IMI Working Paper No. 01/99 - January ISBN 81-87295-05-8

Gupta, Mukul P (2000). "Negative Political Advertising: Some Effects from the 13th Indian General Election 1999" *Global Business Review*. 1(2):249-277. doi:10.1177/097215090000100206

Guttmann, A. (2019) https://www.statista.com/topics/990/global-advertising-market/ accessed on 08 January 2021.

Guttmann, A. (2020) https://www.statista.com/statistics/236943/global-advertising-spending/ accessed on 08 January 2021.

Jack B. Haskins (1964). "Factual Recall as a Measure of Advertising Effectiveness," *Journal of Advertising Research*, 4:7 March

Jones, John Philip (1983). "The Various Roles of Advertising and Their Influence on the Advertising Response function" in *Proceedings of the 1983 convention of the American Academy of Advertising*, p. 143.

Kaldor, N. (1950), "The Economic Aspects of Advertising", *Review of Economic Studies*, Vol. 18, No 1, p. 5

Kenneth, Arrow and George Stigler (1994). Paper for *the Advertising Tax Coalition*, quoted in House Sub-committee on Select Revenue *Measures* of the Committee on Ways and Means, Miscellaneous revenue issues, *Hearings before the Subcommittee on Select Revenue Measures of the Committee on Ways and Means*, 103rd Cong., 1st session, 1994, http://www.archive.org/stream/miscellaneousrev02unit/miscellaneous rev02unit_djvu.txt (accessed December 4, 2020)

Kenneth, Koch (1993). "An Interview With David Kennedy" http://writing.upenn.edu/~afilreis/88/koch.html accessed on 09 January 2020.

Kijewski, Valarie (1982). *Media Advertising When Your Market is in a Recession*, Cambridge, Mass: The Strategic Planning Institute.

Krugman, Herbert E. (1965). "The impact of Television Advertising: Learning Without involvement," *Public Opinion Quarterly*, 29 Fall pp.354-55

Krugman, Herbert E. (1971). "Brain Wave Measures of Media Involvement" *Journal of Advertising Research*, 11:8 February

Krugman, Herbert E. (1977). "Memory without Recall, Exposure Without Perception" *Journal of Advertising Research*, 17-4, August, pp. 7-12.

Krugman, Herbert, E. (1964), "Some Applications of Pupil Measurement" *Journal of Marketing Research*, Nov. pp. 15-19.

Lambin, Jean Jacues (1973). "What is the Real Impact of Advertising", *Harvard Business Review*, Vol. 51, No 3, June, pp. 139-147

Lasker, Albert D (1953). *The Lasker Story*, Chicago: Advertising Publications, Inc. p. 22.

Levitt, Theodore (1969). *The Marketing Mode*, New York: McGraw Hill Book Co., Inc. p. 2

Lipton, Sir Thomas (1931). *Leaves from the Lipton Logs*; London: Hutchinson & Co. Ltd. p.115.

Lloyd, Kaufman (1979). *Perception, the World Transformed*, New York: Oxford University Press, p. 10

Lovell, Mark and Jack Potter (1975). *Assessing the Effectiveness of Advertising*, London: Business Books

Lucas, Darrell Blaine and Steward Handerson Britt (1950). *Advertising Psychology and Research*, New York: McGraw Hill Book Company, Inc. Chap. 1-4.

Lutz, Richard J. (1975), "Changing Brand Attitudes Through Modification of Cognitive Structure," *Journal of Consumer Research* vol. 1 September pp. 49-59.

Lutz, Richard J. (1977). "An Experimental Investigation of Causal Relations Among Cognitions, Affect, and Behavioral Intention" *Journal of Consumer Research*, vol. 3 March pp. 197-208.

Lutz, Richard J. (1978). "Rejoinder" *Journal of Consumer Research*, vol. 4 March pp. 266-71, 276-78.

Lutz, Richard J. and James R. Bettman (1977). "Multiattribute Models in Marketing: A Bicentennial Review" in *Consumer and Industrial buying Behaviour*, A. G. Woodside, Jagdish N. Sheth and P.D. Bennett, eds., New York: North Holland, pp. 137-50.

Mark S. Albion and Paul W. Farris (1979). *Appraising Research On Advertising Economic Impacts*, Cambridge, Mass: Marketing Science Institute, Report #79, 115 p. 131.

Mazis, Michael B. and Janbice E. Adkinson (1976). "An Experimental Evaluation of a Proposed Corrective Advertising Remedy," *Journal of Marketing Research*, vol. 13 May pp. 178-83.

McFadden, Daniel and Train, Kenneth (1996) "Consumers' Evaluation of New Products: Learning from Self and Others" *Journal of Political Economy*, vol. 104-4, pp. 683-703

Michael L. Ray (1973). "Marketing Communication and The Hierarchy of Effects," in *New Models for Communication Research-Sage Annual Reviews of Communication Research Volume II*, Peter Clarke, ed. Beverly Hills: Sage p. 151.

Miniard, Paul W. and Joel B. Cohen (1979). "Isolating Attitudinal and Normative Influences in Behavioral Intentions Models," *Journal of Marketing Research*, vol. 16 February pp. 102-10.

Mitchel, Andrew A., and Jerry C. Olson (1981). "Are Product Attribute Beliefs the Only Mediator of Advertising Effects on Brand Attitudes?" *Journal of Marketing Research*, vol. 18-3 August pp. 318-32

Mitchell, Andrew A. (1979). "Predicting Choice with Preference Functions Estimated from Perceptions of Brands Within a Product Category," in *Analytic Approaches to Product and Marketing Planning*, Allan Shocker, ed. Cambridge, Massachusetts: Marketing Science Institute, pp. 368-87.

Mohan, Manendra (1982). "A Survey of Advertising Themes in 1970's" *Indian Management*, vol. 4, April pp. 39-45

Nelson, Philip (1974) "The Economic Value of Advertising" in *Advertising and Society*, Vale Brozen, ed. New York: New York University Press pp. 43-44.

Nyilasy, Gergely & Reid, Leonard N. (2013) "Agency Practitioner Theories of How Advertising Works" *Journal of Advertising*, 38:3 pp.81-96

Ogilvy, David (1963) *Confessions of an Advertising Man*, New York: Anthenum, republished 2004 London: Southbank pp194

Olson, Jerry C. and Andrew A. Mitchell (1975). "The Process of Attitude Acquisition: The value of a Developmental Approach to Consumer Attitude Research" in *Advances in Consumer Research*, Vol. 2. Mary J Schilinger, ed. Chicago: Association for Consumer Research, pp. 240-64.

Olson, Jerry C., and Philip A. Dover (1976). "Effects of Expectation Creation and Disconfirmation on Belief Elements of Cognitive Structure" in *Advances in Consumer Research*, Vol. 3. Beverly B. Anderson. ed. Cincinnati: Association for Consumer Research, pp. 168-75.

Politz, Alfred (1961). "How Advertising Affects Attitudes & Buying Decisions" in supplement to Vol. VII of *Evaluating Advertising Effectiveness*, Advertising Management Guidebook series, New York: Association of National Advertisers, Inc. p.2.

Ramond, Charles (1970). "Measurement of Sales Effectivess of Advertising" in *Hand Book of Advertising Management*, Roger Burton, ed. New York: McGraw Hill Book Company, pp. 228-9

Rao, Ambar G. and Peter B. Miller (1975) "Advertising/Sales Response Functions", *Journal of Advertising Research*, 15:7, April.

Rosch, Eleanor (1978). "Principles of Categorization" in *Cognition and Categorization* Eleanor Rosch and Barbara B. Lloyds, eds., Hillsdale, New Jersey: Lawrence Elbaum, pp. 27-48.

Scott Walter Dill (1908). *The Psychology of Advertising*, Boston: Small Maynard & Co., p. 221

Shapiro Carl (1980), "Advertising and Welfare: Comment" *The Bell Journal of Economics*, Vol. 11, No. 2 Autumn pp. 749-752

Shocker, Allan D. ed. *Marketing Planning*, 1979, Cambridge, Massachusetts: Marketing Science Institute, pp. 368-87.

Simon, J. L. (1970). "The Effect of Advertising upon Propensity of Consumers", in *Issues in The Economics of Advertising*, Chicago: University of Illinois Press. Chap 9, pp. 193-217

Simon, Julian N. and Johan Arndt (1980). "The Shape of the Advertising Response Function", *Journal of Advertising Research*, 20:23 August.

Socio Economic Effects of Advertising in India, New Delhi: National Council of Applied Economic Research, 1992, p. 1

Spellman, Brian (2015). *If the mind fits, shrink it.* Published January 14th 2015 by lulu.com. ISBN: 1312398647 (ISBN13: 9781312398641)

Starch, Danial (1966). *Measuring Advertising Readership and Results*, New York: McGraw-Hill Book Co. p276.

Steiner, Robert L. (1973). "Does Advertising Lower Consumer Prices" *Journal of Marketing*, Vol. 37, No. 4, October pp. 19-26

Stidsen, Bent (1970). "Some Thoughts on the Advertising Process" *Journal of Marketing*, 34, 1. January 1970, pp. 47 53

Stigler G. J. (1961). "The Economics of Information" *Journal of Political Economy*, 1961

Stivers, Andrew and Tremblay, Victor J. "Advertising, search costs, and social welfare" *Information Economics and Policy*, Volume 17, Issue 3, 2005, pp.317-333

Telser, Lester G. (1964). "Advertising and competition" *Journal of Political Economy*, Vol. 72 No. 6 December pp. 537-62

The Reader's Digest Association (1956) *Lasting Ideas*, New York p. 9

The Works of George Santayana: Soliloquies in England (ed. 1937)

Thomas S. Robertison (1960). "Low Commitment Consumer Behavior" *Journal of Advertising Research* 16:21 April p.88

Thomas, Jerry W. (2020) https://www.decisionanalyst.com/whitepapers/adeffectiveness/ accessed on 05 December 2020.

Tipper, Harry, Harey L Hollingsworth, George B Hotchkiss, Frank A Parsons (1915). *Advertising, Its Principles and Practice*, New York: The Ronald Press Co. p 8.

Tull, D. S., R. A. Boring, and M. H. Gonsior (1964). "A Note on the Relationship of Price and Imputed Quality." *The Journal of Business* vol. 37, no. 2 pp. 186-91

Unwin, Stephen (1972). "A Synchronistic Theory of Advertising" *Journal of Marketing*, vol. 36 No 4 Oct. pp. 16-21.

Vakratsas, Demetrios and Ambler, Tim (1999) "How Advertising Works: What Do We Really Know?" *Journal of Marketing* Vol. 63, No. 1 Jan. pp. 26-43

Vaughm, Richard (1981). "The Consumer Mind- How to Tailor Ad Strategies" *Advertising Age* June pp 45-46.

Wilkie, WIlliam L. and Edgar A. Pessemier (1973) "Issues in Marketing's Use of Multi Attribute Attitude Models" *Journal of Marketing Research*, vol. 10 November pp. 428 41.

William J. McGuire (1978). "An Information Processing Model of Advertising Effectiveness," in Harry L Davis and Alvin J Silk eds. *Behavioral and Management Science in Marketing* New York: Ronald Press, John Wiley & Sons p. 157.

Wittink, Dick R. (1977). "Advertising Increase Sensitivity to Price", *Journal of Advertising Research*, Vol. 17, No. 2, April pp. 39-42.

Wolfe, Harry Dean, James K Brown and G. Clark Thompson (1962). *Measuring Advertising Results*, National Industrial Conference Board, New York, p. 7.

Wolfe, Harry Deane, James K Brown, G. Clark Thompson and, Stephen H Greenberg (1966). *Evaluating Media*, New York: National Industrial Conference Board.

Wright, John S., Daniel S. Warner, Willis L. Winter, Jr., and Sherilyn K. Zeigler (1977). *Advertising*, 4th ed., New York: McGraw Hill.

Wyer, Robert S. (1974). *Cognitive Organisation and Change: An Information Processing Approach*, Hillsdale, New Jersey: Lawrence Erlbaum.

Yuping Liu-Thompkins (2019) A Decade of Online Advertising Research: What We Learned and What We Need to Know, *Journal of Advertising*, 48:1, pp1-13,

Zaveri, Bhawna and Group, "Effect of the Use of Women in Advertising", A Project report of the students of the Advertising and Sales Promotion Management Course, Indian Institute of Management, Ahmedabad, 1982

www.ingramcontent.com/pod-product-compliance
Lightning Source LLC
Chambersburg PA
CBHW072027230526
45466CB00020B/1008